DON JUAN'S WAGER

CULTURAL STUDIES

A series of books edited by Samir Dayal

DON JUAN'S WAGER

François Rachline

TRANSLATED BY

Susan Fairfield

OTHER

OTHER PRESS
New York

Originally published as *Le Pari de Don Juan.*

Copyright © 2001 Presses Universitaires de France

Production Editor: Robert D. Hack

This book was set in 11½ pt. Adobe Caslon by Alpha Graphics of Pittsfield, NH.

10 9 8 7 6 5 4 3 2 1

Library of Congress Cataloging-in-Publication Data

Rachline, François.
  [Pari de Don Juan. English]
  Don Juan's Wager / François Rachline ; translated by Susan Fairfield.
    p. cm.
  Includes bibliographical references and index.
  ISBN 1-892746-80-8
    1. Don Juan (Legendary character) in literature. 2. European literature—History and criticism. 3. Mozart, Wolfgang Amadeus, 1756–1791. Don Giovanni. I. Title.

PN57.D7R3313 2001
809'.93351—dc21

2001021048

To Victor's wife, Hélène K.

CONTENTS

CONTENTS

SERIES EDITOR'S
INTRODUCTION

───══◆══───

*E*ven if we have not arrived at the "end of history," we seem to have arrived at a way station in world history. We are enjoined, rightly or wrongly, to celebrate today the triumph of a globalized culture and of a globalized democratic capitalism. The modular form of that culture and that capitalism, furthermore, goes by the name "America," or EuroAmerica. As if it were a continuation of "The American Century," the new world order returns to us everywhere the images of EuroAmerica—and particularly of American clothing, American forms of culture, American-style advertising, and American ways of doing business and arranging social interaction. Young people, and the not-so-young, have increasingly come to aspire to the same, or to comparable, standards of living, defined by the goods and services one has or commands. In other words, cultures, as well as individuals, take their own measure of success as cultures and individuals in terms of consumption as much as in terms of a "happiness quotient." As François Rachline writes in *Don Juan's Wager*, in this age of advanced capitalism, there is a confusion between having and being—he who does not possess goods can barely be said to exist, or it is as though one exists to the degree that one commands goods and services.

How is it possible to resist this simultaneously oppressive and seductive delusion? Rachline's book posits an alternative erotic economy. And he arrives at his argument through a tour de force that recuperates a romantic and even erotic figure who one might think had fallen out of fashion, or a figure who at the very least had been problematized by feminist discourse. This figure is none other than Don Juan—not just the Don Giovanni of Mozart's opera, but the almost fabulous cultural icon. Yet it is not Don Juan himself whom Rachline wants to reinstate as the unlikely answer to the crassly materialistic view of the "measure of man," but the attitude of Don Juan, which Rachline terms *giovannism*.

One could object that Rachline's giovannism participates nevertheless in a phallic economy and does not merely offer an alternative erotic economy, but is simply a reactionary backlash. For does a celebration of Don Juan's attitude not invite condemnation, given the devaluation of women implied by this attitude? The name of Don Juan has a rather bad odor today, particularly in some academic circles. And even in the popular imagination, he is seen as a figure to be derided as a representative of unctuous machismo or as a misogynist masquerading as a ladies' man.

Let it be granted that giovannism is coded as a masculine attitude even if ultimately in this book it is generic terminology, clearly not intended to exclude women. It would, however, be a serious misreading to think that Rachline's giovannism is a throwback to the type of the "ladies' man." No serious observer of contemporary society could place such a notion at the center of an analytic model of cultural practice in the face of all the advances feminism has introduced into the discourses of sexuality or gender. Rachline is adequately familiar with contemporary sexual politics not to make his goal merely the rehabilitation of Don Juan's devalued reputation. In the first place, it is more a generalized savoir vivre and a general attitude to human and property relations that interest Rachline. He sees in Don Juan a figure of a certain elegance and courage, someone who speaks to our time of mass-mediated globalization. It is bourgeois symbolic capital, and the social structures and illusions supporting bourgeois forms of life, that giovannism most powerfully subverts. In referring particularly to Mozart, the author breathes new life into the rather hoary operatic personage of Don Giovanni, who seems to belong to an earlier age, and offers a fascinating case study of an orientation to life in which love and even death take on a new cast. Giovannism is a celebration of love, not irresponsibility in love. Through a refusal to repay what one owes, the contemporary attitude of giovannism is paradoxically an opening to the other, a sustaining of the interdependence of human beings in social relationships. And most powerfully and stirringly, it points to an openness to death that refreshes life in refusing to be cowed before the constraints that bourgeois society enshrines as morality.

The "Postscript" places the whole text sharply into a contemporary perspective. Here it becomes most powerfully clear that the thesis of giovannism is for the author a way of conceptualizing the relation of the individual (subjective/ human) and the economic and therefore a different way of conceptualizing the contemporary operation of capital. If we think of giovannism as a mode of being a citizen/ subject in contemporary global culture, we can understand it as a principle from which one can proceed to assign value to the various situations life presents, to sexual or gender relations, to goods, to social interactions with other human beings. In other words, implicit in such an analysis is the category of the *ethical*, as well as the *libidinal*. But what kind of ethics does a giovannist "valuation" imply?

As against the lust for accumulating material goods and tokens of power to shore up the increasingly fragile sense of self that is left to us in the age of late capitalism (according to theorists such as Fredric Jameson, for instance), giovannism recognizes that "dwelling," or stasis, is death, and possession is a form of death. The alternative to death offered by Don Juan is an embrace of the state of being perpetually in debt. When he tailors himself according to the image of giovannism, the contemporary subject—and par excellence the modern entrepreneur and the type of modern individual Rachline dubs the *homo internetus*—does not live according to the logic of accumulation. Instead of seeking safety and security, instead of capitulating to the anxiety to guarantee a predictable future by amassing financial and other capital, giovannism embraces the *promesse aléatoire*, the aleatory promise synecdochically encapsulated in the example of Options and Futures. On the personal level it signifies a preference for the promissory over the permanent. As projected into the context of a global economy, it describes a parallel with a nation-state's readiness to remain in debt or to be comfortable with a deficit; it captures a new appetite for the instabilities of a global market economy rather than an anxiety to protect a national economy's self-sufficiency.

And if contemporary ("postmodern") life has led to the increasing robotization of the human, giovannism allows us to recognize a possibility even in this sorry state of affairs. For when we cede repetition (repetitive modes such as assembly-line production) to the province of the machine, then the singular can become more properly the realm of the truly human, and thus make the human freer. This is one of Rachline's genuinely bracing and refreshing ideas. Very few cultural critics have written as provocatively as Rachline has in the postscript about the new kind of economic good, namely, information, which it is impossible to accumulate. The dominant idea, at least in the cultural studies departments of the United States, is that the era of late capitalism and now globalization is characterized by flexible accumulation. And it is in this context that the book makes an extremely powerful intervention into (especially American) cultural studies. In short, this book suggestively links the economic, the libidinal, and the ethical as dimensions of citizenship, and raises questions about how we might want to rethink these interlinked modes of citizenship that are available to a subject in a global cultural economy.

Samir Dayal

PREFACE

Why does Don Juan continue to attract us? Four centuries have not dulled his glamour: surely this is surprising. Even if sexuality is obviously his most spectacular dimension, it is perhaps not the one that intrigues us the most today.[1] With the benefit of hindsight, we really ought to investigate more fully what his behavior tells us about ourselves and our culture. If Don Juan had disappeared with his time, he would represent an era, and his figure would sum up a vision of the world. His libertinism would be enough to define him, and we would have to give up trying to find in him the characteristics of a culture. He would have turned into an anecdote.

But this is not the case. He has come down to us in a state of freshness that is truly astonishing; he is still relevant and continues to work in the shadow and the uncon-

---

1. In his *History of Sexuality*, Michel Foucault (1976) emphasizes that ever since the seventeenth century sexuality has not been repressed but, on the contrary, fully expressed, studied in depth, inventoried, exploited, unveiled, and analyzed, all of this through very different legal mechanisms. According to Foucault, Don Juan overturns "the two great systems conceived by the West for governing sex: the law of marriage and the order of desires" and is "driven, in spite of himself, by the . . . madness of sex" (pp. 19–20).

scious of Western thought. In this sense, he is not just a literary character but a major feature of civilization.

The figure of Don Juan arises in the beginning of the seventeenth century. At this time, he is a criminal, a deceiver, a liar, an impostor. His acts threaten the established order. He is a menace to society. Cowardly, manipulative, wicked: there are so many adjectives to define him. The eighteenth century puts the finishing touches on this portrait by adding *hypocritical* and *cynical* to the list but also makes him into a strange hero. He embodies the free individual confronting society, exploit and experimentation, the flourishing and apotheosis of the subject. These are his high points. The nineteenth century portrays his aging and decline. He becomes a bourgeois worn out by life, disappointed, haunted by unfulfilled desire. The twentieth century makes him a figure of fun and yet does not nullify him. His shoulders are bent by the weight of his past. His laughter has become uneasiness. He is a sorry figure, adrift, ill, a case to be seized upon by psychoanalysis. He is no longer much of a threat at all: religion no longer structures existence, debt is a commonplace of capitalism, procreation and sexual pleasure are unlinked, adultery is amusing, honor takes on an antiquated charm.

Do his avatars leave him a future? At this moment when we are beginning a still virginal century, I do think it is possible to think of Don Juan without heaping sarcasm on him and without condemning him a priori, without either ennobling or debasing him, without idealizing or demonizing him. For us today he is much more of a concept than a figure.

In the *Trickster of Seville*, the first play in which the character appears on the Western stage, Tirso de Molina (1625) tries to defend Christian society through an account of the punishment associated with transgression. A propaganda device in the service of the economic and social organization founded on monogamy, the play shows the madness that could destroy the Western order if the excesses represented by Don Juan were not hunted down. Only the tragic death of the seducer permits the restoration of the rules he scorned. And his most severe punishment is not mere death—which is, after all, an entirely human episode—but the penalty to which it leads, eternal damnation. Thus we have the contract imagined by Christianity: either a quiet, honest, pious, charitable life and the hope of paradise, or an agitated, dissolute, impious, egotistic life and the certainty of hell.

A one-man transgression business, Don Juan acts as a revealer. From the epistemological point of view adopted here, this figure, as it were, sets forth the negative of the Christian order that produced him. Read him in reverse and you will see affirmed, as if laid bare, some of the greatest principles of Western society of the second millennium: believe in God, marry once, forbid adultery, respect your word of honor, pay your debts, fear death. This book is an attempt to shed light on the common basis of these values that secretly governs the architecture whose keystones they are. Don Juan does not affirm them; he denies them, and in so doing he tells us about ourselves. Observing him amounts to looking at our culture in a mirror.

The ground in which our current ideas grow is also where we find the foundations of our thought. Even if it is illusory to imagine that we can reveal them in their entirety, at least we should try to investigate our most hidden beliefs. Prominent among them is balance, the promoter of symmetry. This organizing concept, this major paradigm, is in itself one of the great adventures of Western thought, one, incidentally, whose history remains to be written. Little by little it has invaded all fields of knowledge, whether the oldest disciplines like medicine and physics, where its reign has lasted for centuries, or the comparatively young human sciences, especially economics, where it still asserts an imperial presence.

In this book Don Juan is the guiding thread of a meditation on the central infrastructure of the notion of balance, of symmetrical reciprocity. When both the individual and society as a whole call for equivalence and just compensation, he symbolizes deviance. He understands neither the logic nor the practice of balance but remains a stranger to them. To this prudent world he opposes a disconcerting economy in which compensation is not legal tender. An economy of the wide-open gap. A poetic economy. In all his relations with other people or with God—love, exchange, commitment, gift-giving, debt, death—his incorrigible asymmetry prevails. This is his wager.

ACKNOWLEDGMENTS

Like my preceding books, this one owes a great deal to the presence and the encouragement of Dominique, Julie, and Guillaume.

Some of my closest friends favored my manuscript with their careful reading before publication. I very much want to express my appreciation for their support and for the efforts they encouraged me to make. May the painter, the mathematician, the anthropologist, and the philosopher find here a further sign of my gratitude and my friendship.

In accordance with the rightly hallowed formula, I of course claim sole responsibility for the result.

PART I

FIGURES

ONE

WORDS

$\mathcal{F}$or several hundred years a strange figure has permeated the Western imaginary and left deep marks there. But his heritage, if I may use that term, remains complex. On the one hand, at the dawn of our modernity and as if anticipating its later expansion, we have the assertion of the power of desire and the imperatives of the body. On the other hand, the rejection of any symmetrical reciprocity actually negates what was to become a Western society won by the values of a triumphant economy. Both movements go together. It is even possible that they actually maintain one another by a mutual counterbalancing. The first movement makes our figure a precursor; the second makes him an exception. But the precursor is an unwitting one, since he is not a model and is hardly revered by a history in which he participates despite himself. As for the exception, it works in the shadows and little by little infiltrates a world that nevertheless rejects it.

An anarchist *avant la lettre*, Don Juan resists any compromise and, in his actions, proclaims the freedom of the individual. But we must never forget that these actions are fictive and belong to the waking dream of a society reflecting on itself. Granting primacy to the body, this kind of being is no longer a means to expression through discourse but an end in itself, shouting out its joy in life. A lonely figure in the midst of the din that surrounds him, Don Juan prefigures the explosion of sheer individual power. He shatters the social order that establishes and distributes roles once and for all. Women were enclosed in economic and sexual frameworks—he breaks the latter through desire for the former. Men were prudently connected to one another within social relations fixed by rank, honor, and the disposition of property—he dissolves this stability. Sacred rules imposed the domination of God—he laughingly profanes them. But, although he anticipates a later evolution that will gradually affect all Western societies, he does not set out to be a hero. He breaks chains but does not build. He never gets more than halfway through. Like Pangloss in Voltaire's *Candide*, he could maintain that all is for the best in the best of all possible worlds. But Pangloss had only one eye, and half of reality escaped him. Against the imperatives of society Don Juan sets only his own personal demands. His body governs his mind, and this is how he stands apart from all of Western history. All he has to offer is the sheer enjoyment of each moment. At the same time, he cannot be reduced to a mere consumer of women, since he does not just aspire to carnal pleasure (Sade, for example, did a better job of that) but also claims his freedom over against society. Over against society, not for society or in it. And this is the heart of the matter.

Devouring prohibitions, he treated himself to what amounts to a feast on a historic scale, and in so doing he launched across the centuries a process of questioning the very foundations of our thought. He expressed the power of that thought and marked its limits. His glorification of the self, shown most fully in his rejection of symmetrical reciprocity, projected him beyond his own time. This is surely why this adventurer of the unthinkable continues to speak of us and to us.

"Us" means the West, that sphere that is not confined to a geographical space but is part of the world of thought, one of whose great ambitions is to reveal its own illusions. Don Juan goes about this task without knowing it, without wishing it, and in fact without being able to accomplish it. In his actions, he continually rejects one of the most strongly affirmed beliefs in our mental universe, the idea that a kind of necessary compensation must govern all the actions of life in society. This credo, which was gradually established as an automatic given in the awareness of modern man, is an expression of a philosophical atmosphere in which Judaism is criticized by its natural child, Christianity.

The Torah, the Hebraic law, posed the question of choice in broad terms. Ever since man ate from the tree of good and evil, he lost his innocence, gaining in freedom but also discovering the anxiety associated with choice. The biblical text does not say that the tree gives man the knowledge of what good and evil are, just that it becomes possible to differentiate between these two categories. Conscience is thus opened to the idea of an alternative. The anxiety of choosing evil in the place of good, and vice versa, constrains man even if there are many intermediate cases: doing good in a good way, doing good in an evil way, doing evil in an evil way, and doing evil in a good way.[1]

The dilemma is close to Pascal's (1662) famous wager, since there is no way that choice can be avoided. Not choosing is a choice in itself and thus belongs to the set of all possible choices. This alternative could be annulled if man had eternity before him, which would amount to eating of the tree of life and death. What would it matter, in that case, if he made the wrong choices, since he would have all the time he needed to revise them? Spinoza (1677) rightly criticized theology because of its confusion between obedience to a moral law and knowledge itself. If Adam confuses the interdiction of the tree with the knowledge of good and evil, misfortune is definitely in store for him. On the other hand, understanding that the tree contains something bad for him should enable him to live in search of what is good. The knowledge of the difference between good and evil is based not on a moral law imposed by authority but on the understanding of man himself that this difference is essential to the determination of what is good and what is bad for him. If this choice did not exist, what would human actions be worth?

To be sure, man tasted of the tree of knowledge, but this transgression did not give rise to a cataclysm. He now knows of the existence of good and evil, and that is all. His "fall into time" thus occurs from the moment he can no longer

---

1. Concrete situations could be multiplied indefinitely: doing good in a quite evil way, doing evil in a rather good way, and so forth.

feel the temptation of eternal life. In other words, there is no sin; there is a privation.

Paul of Tarsus does not share this sentiment. In his Letter to the Romans he speaks of an original sin that, on the whole, remains rather vague. As a Jew, he judged more or less confusedly that his people had killed God, a hypothesis that Freud (1939), in *Moses and Monotheism*, fully examined when he found in this line of thought the sign of a possible return of the repressed. Paul found the weight of this murder unbearable and proposed a founding interpretation of Christianity in terms of a personal sacrifice that would be liberating. He thereby established something radically new. This was the beginning of a dominant vision of symmetry and compensation for every deviation, which would prevail even if that compensation were rejected ad infinitum.

In Judaism, the divine breath opens to the world, opens the world, opens onto the world. There are none of the cataclysms or terrible upheavals generally attributed to a Zeus or a thundering Jupiter, just a few words uttered to create the world, almost in a whisper: "Let there be light."[2] To this delicate and fragile origin there corresponds an

---

2. The biblical formula is more complex, since it uses the "conversive *vav*," a letter that can change a future into a past and a past into a future when it is attached to a verb as a prefix. This linguistic feature does not occur in the Indo-European languages, and, according to Professor Jacob Klein of Bar-Ilan University, is found, outside of Hebrew, in two other Semitic languages, Phoenician and Moabitic. The passage from Genesis would have to be translated as something like "May the light that was in the past be in the future," unless we keep in mind that the present "Let there be light" immediately implies the complement "now and eternally."

original final end, the coming of the Messiah. This is a fascinating idea when considered from the perspective of a philosophy of becoming, not from the perspective of the hope of a final revelation. The mathematician Didier Dacunha-Castelle (1996) notes in this connection that, for Messianism, the future is something between tomorrow and never. This conclusion that is indefinitely postponed is like the abolition of a conclusion. The original breath, the word, opens onto the world but above all creates an open world. A kind of gradient is established. Nothing balances or compensates the origin.

Pauline thought introduces what Judaism leaves out: to original sin viewed as a debt contracted toward God, the sacrifice brings a perfect reply. It settles the debt. Man is saved. Through the death of Christ, Paul announces, we are present at the cancellation of a debt that Judaism never managed to pay. This burden that a whole people bore for centuries without ever being able to get free of it was purely and simply abolished by the advent of Christianity. To this end Paul emphasized the original burden, to be sure, but at the same time he augmented the power of the redemption.

Let us not argue here about the validity of such a thesis. What matters, I suggest, is the grand idea promoted by the new Pauline philosophy, one that was destined to structure the world of Western thought: it is not only possible to pay the debt, but this act reestablishes the divine balance that man upset. Good and evil are strictly opposed, the former being able to compensate for the latter. The entire doctrine of the redemption challenges the gap, accepted by Judaism, in which one could envision an open process of becoming. By making Christ the son of God, and a god himself, Paul's proposal accomplishes a real tour de force, one that aroused Nietzsche's extreme amazement: "God sacrificing himself for the guilt of man, God paying himself off, God as the sole figure who can redeem on man's behalf that which has become irredeemable for man himself—the creditor sacrificing himself for his debtor, out of *love* (are we supposed to believe this?)—out of love for his debtor!" (1886, p. 72).[3]

With Paul, payment is made through the Christian sacrifice and saves mankind from the Law, which was responsible for transgression (cf. Romans 5:13). In other words, Faith saves from the Law, and only faith in Jesus Christ can settle all accounts. Thus an account will be kept of all your acts: the wicked will be punished, the good rewarded. The former will know the pangs of hell, the latter the delights of heaven. The last shall be first and vice versa. God is a scrupulous accountant. He will know how to restore the balance.

---

3. How much more would this philosopher have been astonished to learn that it is possible to address God as a creditor, the way Yossel Rakover does as he dies fighting! As presented by Zvi Kolitz (1995) in the guise of a manuscript dated April 28, 1943 and found in the rubble of the Warsaw Ghetto, here is an extract from this fiction that is as true as reality: "After everything I have lived through, I cannot say that my relationship to God remains unchanged, but I can say with absolute certainty that my belief in Him has not changed a hair's breadth. In the past, when I was well and well off, my relation to God was as to one who kept on granting me favors for which I was always indebted; now my relationship to Him is as to one who owes me something, owes me much. And since I feel that He owes me something, I believe that I have the right to demand it of Him" (p. 17).

The Christian matrix of the idea that governs the existence of Don Juan thus forms a mental structure within which this figure's subversive strategy is located. In the perfectly balanced universe, nothing can happen in one direction that is not compensated by an event in the opposite direction. Death offsets life. Punishment offsets fault. Payment offsets debt. Hell offsets heaven. A general system of compensations operates in secret. It defines the contours of a morality that maintains a vast double-entry bookkeeping that forbids lasting depressions. Imbalances are temporary. If Don Juan transgresses the law of equality, he can do so only intermittently. If he manages to break out of the rigid constraints imposed by the law of equivalence, he will have to pay later on. "An eye for an eye" does not mean that compensation takes place instantly. It can be deferred, but it will happen no matter what. And yet Don Juan does not take into account the warnings and threats that society rains down on him. He dismisses them with a confident tongue. Nothing and no one can exercise the least power over him. He is; the rest is nonsense. And so, if he reveals to us what we are by saying, through his actions, what we do not manage to be, his words should be lodged in those critical regions where they will be side by side with the relation to God, to death, to time, to desire, to the other. His wager constantly involves a strategy of rupture—a strategy that is also made up of ruptures.

TWO

PERSONNE*

To get to the wager whose vanishing lines Don Juan draws in his acts presupposes an encounter with the figure himself. But this figure is not easy to grasp or to bring onstage. He takes so many forms that he is almost impossible to represent.

Why this difficult access? Why can't one simply have an idea of the character, social status, and even the physical appearance of Don Juan?

Although he is constant in his inconstancy, he has none of the stubbornness of a Sisyphus. Although he casts a jaded eye on the world, he never experiences the sadness of a Faust. Although he is convivial, the earthiness of a Cyrano is completely unlike him. Although he perseveres in each of his undertakings, his has none of the tenacity of a Prometheus. Although he is an enthusiastic lover, the passion of a Tristan

---

*Translator's note: "nobody" in French is *personne*, which also means "person." This dual meaning underlies the present chapter.

does not come close to him. Although he makes light of the world, he lacks the mad inspiration of a Don Quixote. Although he pursues his pleasure, the self-centeredness of a Narcissus is alien to him. Although he takes on many guises, he escapes the schizophrenia of a Jekyll. Although he ends dramatically, his life lacks the tragic dimension of an Oedipus. Although he cannot bear to wait, he does not know the impatience of a Hamlet.

Who is he, then? A great lord who enjoys himself (Da Ponte/ Mozart), or a damned soul of royalty beneath his rags (Verlaine)? A wealthy descendent of conquerors (Tirso de Molina), or a libertine gentleman experiencing monetary difficulties (Molière)? The Devil incarnate (Jules Barbey d'Aurevilly), or a calm hero (Baudelaire)? A Southerner without stature (Montherlant), or a great wildman of the Renaissance (Jean-Victor Hocquard)? A homosexual unbeknownst to himself (Marañon), or the women's whore (Joseph Delteil)? A lethal eroticist (Pierre Jean Jouve), or a vulgar destroyer of marriage (Pushkin)? A psychotic (Sándor Ferenczi), or the liberator of Woman (Otto Rank)? An illusionist (Ramon del Valle Inclàn), or a victim of womanhood (George Bernard Shaw)? A man athirst for the infinite (Alfred de Musset) or crazed by beauty (E. T. A. Hoffmann), a repentant monster (Zorilla), a prey to petticoats (Nelly Kaplan), an idealist (Lenau), a geometer (Max Frisch), a monk of love (Félicien Marceau), women's dream (Denis de Rougement), a super-male (Alfred Jarry), a dandy (Lord Byron), a pervert (Michel Foucault)? An absurd man (Albert Camus)? Is he all of this at the same time, or none of this? I am breaking off the catalogue here so as not to weary the reader. But it could be greatly extended in view of the fact that this figure inspired a wide range of artists, as well as writers, poets, composers, filmmakers, and painters, not to mention philosophers, essayists, and linguists. Who in the West does not have a *Don Juan* in the desk drawers of his imagination? This observation alone justifies our investigating the attraction that this figure has exercised for so long on our thought.

Some have compared Don Juan to Casanova, finding in the splendid Italian a sort of archetype of the seducer,[1] but the similarity hardly stands up to even a superficial analysis. The figure of Don Juan existed well before the life of Casanova became the talk of the town, and it takes only a glance into the latter's autobiography to understand that worlds separate the two men. While Casanova is able to retrace his life through his multiple adventures with women, Don Juan never relates anything, because he has no History, only histories.

Others believe they find his incarnation in the less renowned figure of a Spanish gentleman, a certain Don Miguel de Mañara. This founder of the Hospital of Charity in Seville, where his portrait by Juan Valdés Leal can be admired today, dreamed that he was present at his own burial and immediately converted. Repentant, he entirely changed

---

1. Especially since, at the very beginning of his autobiography, Casanova (1788) mentions among his ancestors a certain Don Jacobe Casanova, who abducted a certain Dona Ana Palafox the day after she made her vows and whose uncle was a certain Don Jouan Casanova!

his ways and transformed his dissolute life into a holy one. This example is often used as an excuse by Christians to show that everything must be paid for in this world and that God pardons those who beseech him, even *in extremis*.

Instead of incarnating Don Juan, aren't these images oversimplified? They would be touching if they did not reveal what is inaccessible in the figure. To reach Don Juan, is it really enough to add up the list of his character traits? Would we have to include all the features mentioned by Balzac, Théophile Gautier, Tolstoy, George Sand, Goldoni, Ghelderode, Gendarme de Bevotte, Gazanizza, Glück, Stravinsky, Richard Strauss, Ferucio Busoni, Bertold Brecht, François Truffaut, Rembrandt, Fragonard, Delacroix, Lacan, Michel Foucault, Michel Serres, Gilles Deleuze, Michel Butor, Maurice Blanchot, Georges Bataille, and so many others?

Would the sum of these distinctive signs be an accurate portrait? Nothing could be less certain. An individual never yields himself up as a totality, nor can he be seen in the entirety of his aspects. In most cases, the angle chosen to depict him conceals dimensions that a different viewpoint would undoubtedly have revealed. Man is not one of those objects of which a mobile camera could make a complete image by circling around it. What we reveal of ourselves to another is what his presence impels us to offer him, and vice versa. If, then, man is already an almost inaccessible combinatory, what shall we say about a figure like Don Juan?

Does this mean that we have to give up on a total portrait and approach him bit by bit? It so happens that apparently insignificant details express what is essential about him more than grand descriptions that aspire to completeness. Thus Prosper Mérimée (1910) states that Don Juan smokes cigars. Despite its appearance of superficiality, this single remark may say more about the figure than long speeches about his costumes, his high forehead, his proud gaze, his haughty bearing, his corpulence or slimness. Isn't a cigar like the river of which Heraclitus says that we never step in it twice? Isn't it the symbol of a beginning that is always begun all over again? Can't a good Havana also serve as a metaphor for sexual pleasure? Isn't the closeness of *consumption* and *consummation* obvious? Don't we always have to light another cigar and keep on renewing this operation to find again and again a pleasure that will never be either entirely the same or entirely different? And besides, doesn't Molière (1665) begin his *Dom Juan* with the praise of tobacco?

Other, more striking, details could be added. Though Don Juan laughs uproariously, though he unfailingly laughs at himself, though laughter can always be seen behind his eyes, he never causes anyone to laugh at *him*. Though he is flamboyant and merry, he causes neither merriment nor flamboyance in others. He himself may enjoy acting the comedian, whether in derision or in a kind of self-irony, but no one around him and no one accompanying him dares to forget the premonition or prediction of a drama. Even if everything seems to suggest that Don Juan has no knowledge of the fatal outcome, this hypothesis hardly stands up to examination. Like everyone, he is aware that he must die, but he gives no sign of destructive doubt or paralyzing interrogation. Does he live on that impossibility of living that the poet Edmond Jabès (1991) speaks about, an impossibility that death makes possible by setting a limit to it? He knows what he wants, where he is going, and how to get there. He inspires fear even as he exerts an irresistible attraction. He frightens and seduces at one and the same time. This ambivalence emphasizes the difficulty of creating a psychological portrait.

In fact, neither the global approach nor the sequence of details really gives access to this figure. If a psychological portrait turns out to be unlikely, a physical one is just as difficult to draw. It seems that the figure of Don Juan is endlessly eluding us. Why? Perhaps because he has no name and wears a mask.

The first scene of Tirso de Molina's *The Trickster of Seville* (1625) takes place in the bedroom of Isabela, the daughter of the Governor of Seville. A man has sneaked in. He makes believe he is her lover. Isabela asks his name. He answers, "I'll tell you who I am. I am a man who's nameless" (p. 5). When King Alfonso, informed of the crime, comes into Isabela's room and questions the intruder, he hears that no one is present but "a man and a woman" (p. 7).

Right from the beginning, then, Don Juan is just a figurehead. Is it just a coarse joke on the part of the monk Gabriel Tellez, alias Tirso de Molina, the spiritual father of the hero, to saddle him with the name *Don Juan* that evokes the *Juan*, or the diminutive *Juanito*, designating the male sexual organ in Spanish? In any case, this is a man without a name who bursts onto the universal stage, in contrast to all the great figures of the Western imagination who are marked with the seal of their patronymic. While all of these others lay a strong claim to their names as a tie to their lineage, an affirmation of their character, and a social inscription, Don Juan remains entirely circumspect in this regard.

The lack of a patronymic prevents, or nearly prevents, us from identifying an individual. If you don't know someone's name, can you tell where he comes from, what he does, who his ancestors were, and where he belongs? A man without a name is like a man without a shadow: he is not truly a man but a pathetic guy, a nothing. In the view of society, a man without a name does not exist. To the ritual formula of the judge in the course of a deposition: "name, age, profession," Don Juan's answer would be a threefold "none." The name is a guide, something to hang onto, a project and a root, and it sometimes determines a man's fate, even though, ultimately, we know nothing about him when all we know is his name. This first attribution of birth, this existential singularity, is missing for Don Juan. The lack marks him from the outset with the seal of the unknown.

The brief exchange between the King and Don Juan in the *Trickster* also recalls the dialogue between Moses and God. When the prophet is about to embark on the great adventure that will change human thought and overturn human history, he questions his credibility among the Hebrews. God has designed Moses' mission and repeatedly assures his prophet that he will always be at his side and ahead of his words, but Moses mentions one of his numerous hesitations: What if the people to whom I am going to speak ask me your name, he asks God, what shall I answer? Now the God of Israel has no other name than the unpronounceable tetragrammaton, YHWH. Moses will have to make do with an answer that eludes questioning: *Ehyeh asher ehyeh*: "I shall be who I shall be."[2] The absence of the patronymic here is the absolute mark of divinity. Only God cannot be named. An unnamable and invisible God, omnipresent by the very fact of this strange absence, has what it takes to make an impression on men. A man who refuses to name himself, who offers a new face at every encounter: Is he a man? From his very first word, Don Juan knows how to place himself at a distance from men. He is somewhere between the human and the divine. In the penumbra in which he remains when the king is about to unmask him, he can be scornful, for who would recognize him? He will escape, slip away between the fingers of his pursuers, remain anonymous. Because this is his great concern: anonymity. In order to run after women, seduce them, love them, to avoid fatal indiscretions, he can't afford to be recognized; in fact, he tries to be misrecognized. And so it is not surprising when Don Juan refuses to give his name to Isabela.

Furthermore, Molière's Dom Juan,[3] and the Don Giovanni of Da Ponte/ Mozart have to resort to subterfuge when they find they have been discovered. In the Molière

---

2. Exodus 3:13–14. The usual translation is "I am that I am," whereas the Hebrew text uses the future and not the present.

3. This is Molière's spelling; in what follows I shall use the standard form for the sake of simplicity.

play, the seducer launches on a complicated explanation, in which his eagerness to get rid of Elvire competes with a hypocritical homage to religion. Don Giovanni tries to pass the woman off as crazy, since only a madwoman would claim to recognize a man who has no name!

Who is hiding behind this figurehead? No one knows, since he tries not only to remain anonymous but to conceal his real self. Don Juan is never knowable, or, a fortiori, recognizable, because he always wears a mask—"mask" in both its original and its metaphorical meanings. If the man stepped forth in broad daylight, unmasked, he would reveal his identity. The mask sustains the doubt associated with difference. His face must remain inaccessible. To be sure, he can get taken for a coward, but what does this matter to him? He always pursues the same end: not to be discovered. The ghost of Don Gonzalo, the Commandant whom Don Juan killed in a duel when he tried to intervene to defend his daughter, accuses him of cowardice because he ran away after killing him. If I ran away, Don Juan explains, it was to avoid being recognized.

And it is not just a case of defying men. Death is also defied. Linda, the girl seduced by the aged Don Juan of Montherlant (1972), begs him to take off his mask. And the seducer replies that he is keeping it on so that death will not recognize him.

Like makeup, the mask attracts but deceives, emphasizes but falsifies, disguises but expresses, exposes but conceals. It is the attribute of someone who never reveals himself and who confronts reality in the name of imagination. It bears witness to the interpenetration of the two worlds. Whereas a carnival mask hides a person who is ready to unmask if necessary, behind Don Juan's mask is another mask, which covers a third, and so on. In the last scene of Montherlant's play, the hero is preparing to flee the pack of self-righteous pursuers. Before leaving his house, he puts on a mask. His son cries out in fright, because the features of death have appeared on his father's face. Don Juan then tries to remove the death-mask but is unable to do so: mask and skin are one. And so it is masked death who rushes out into the street. Even though Montherlant claimed that this was just a theatrical notion, its symbolic force is striking. Among all of Don Juan's faces, the face of death was awaiting its time. And so the hero will wear a mask for all eternity. Inscrutable in his lifetime, he remains so after his death.

In Book 9 of Homer's *Odyssey*, Polyphemus asks Ulysses what his name is. Ulysses replies, "Nobody [*Personne*]" (pp. 366–367). When the Cyclops is asked who blinded him, he naturally gives this name, one that is associated with all the possibilities of the human race and the complete absence of anyone. A *personne* can be anybody. *Personne* is nothing.[4]

Personne comes from the Latin *persona*, which means "theatrical mask." To be a person and to be masked amounts to the same thing. More than any other man, Don Juan

---

4. The concept of *personne* is very broad. As Jorge Luis Borges (1967) notes, "to be one thing is inexorably not to be all other things; the confused intuition of this truth has induced men to imagine that not to be is more than to be something, and that, in some way, it is to be everything" (p. 120).

has no true face, only faces, multiple reflections of his identities. The man without a face is also the man with a hundred faces. Each time one of them is uncovered, another appears as if in a double exposure. Don Juan never takes his mask off. We have to listen to Debussy's *Masques* to get an idea of the agitated movement that produces this uninterrupted sequence, in which the impression of breathless pursuit seems unending.

A man without a name, he is neither citizen nor subject, merely a subjectivity without a project. A masked man, he evades himself and others. A man without a name, a masked man, Don Juan is thus *personne*, nobody. Elusive in life, he also escapes death's grasp—and so in fact he does not die but disappears. No tomb for the man without a name, no face for the masked man. Always hidden behind the absence that alone enables him to exist. Why should we be surprised, then, if we cannot describe him? Montherlant's Commandant describes him to his wife, the Countess, in a way that is reminiscent of Orson Welles's portrayal of Citizen Kane: he's a great guy and a rotten bastard, a lover and a pig, a man of honor and a criminal, an exceptional person and a person of no stature. *Personne*: a person and a nobody. Everything and nothing.

We may add that, since his handsomeness is irrelevant to our reflection, we may as well imagine him ugly.

THREE

CONCEPTUAL FIGURE

*W*ords betraying speech and acts transgressing social prohibitions: Could Don Juan have something in common
with mythical figures? Do we find in him one of the rare
myths of the Christian West?

Oedipus, Sisyphus, and Prometheus clearly belong to the
mythical domain, but Don Juan? Ever since the nineteenth
century invented the term *donjuanism* to describe men's
behavior toward women, the idea has developed of a particular myth directly associated with the exclusive pursuit of
carnal pleasure. The figure of the seducer is unknown in
ancient civilizations, and although Greece and Rome tell
stories of the escapades of certain gods, the heroes of an-
tiquity know nothing of the body's insatiable quest. That
restless search is a modern notion.

When Don Juan emerges into Western thought, he
exists right from the beginning as an exception, to be sure,
but also as an individual marked by everything this regi-
mented culture censures: lying, attempted rape, flight,

murder, unbelief, refusal to make amends, nonpayment of debts. As a transgressor he joins all mythic heroes, who face the task of resolving the conflicts that ordinary mortals come up against but cannot master.

But the sources of a myth are lost in the darkness of time, and this is not the case for Don Juan. The date and place of birth of Prometheus, who stole fire from Zeus and gave it to men, are unknown. We do not know the origin of Sisyphus, who was the King of Corinth and yet a poor wretch condemned to push a rock up a hill only to have it roll back down just as it was about to reach the top. As for Oedipus, he would never have become so famous if Freud had not pulled him out of the rubble of the imagination, in which he had been buried. Can Don Juan claim this kind of status? Is it possible to compare this quite recent figure to his celebrated forebears? If so, should we classify him with so-called primitive narratives? Are there analogies among the Nambikwara analyzed by Lévi-Strauss, or among Malinowski's Trobriand Islanders?

If Don Juan is mythic, is his an etiological story, in which we hear of beings who were alive at a time so far back that it is inaccessible to historical research, as Mircea Eliade has suggested, a story that reveals the historical anchoring points of the West? Does it represent a stage in the inexorable march of thought from magic to reason, in accordance with the outdated evolutionism of Frazer? Or is it instead, following Lévi-Strauss, about a language, an architecture that is stable and identifiable behind its poetic variations and that informs us about the structures of the society in which it arose? Are we witnessing the emergence onto the stage of awareness of a subterranean, unconscious, inexplicable thought arising from time immemorial, as Carl Jung would argue? Is the story of Don Juan simply transmitting a genesis in codified form, the real but disguised account of an original murder perpetrated by those who narrate it, as the interpretation of myths put forth by René Girard would have it? Is it expressing ideas in a form that is strange, certainly, but nevertheless instructive because it "says something about something," to use Paul Ricoeur's phrase? Or is it, finally, a charming story, more or less far-fetched, a poetic production with no true bearing on the lived reality of men, as might be claimed by the extreme rationalism found in the great critical works of Marx on society, Nietzsche on morals, Freud on the psyche?

Something of the figure is to be found in each of these interpretations, but none of them is able to define him. Surely it is hard to maintain that Don Juan unfolds a grand narrative of origins, since his own origin has a historical date. Jean Rousset (1990), who does not doubt the mythic nature of Don Juan, has even analyzed its genesis on the basis of key constitutive elements. In his view, a popular legend of the Christian West and a theological debate lie behind the stock motifs of the dead man who punishes, the rather featherbrained leading man who goes against the law and demonstrates his inconstancy, and a series of women who give credence to this last aspect.

If the origin is known, can we still speak of myth? And yet one of the ingredients of myth does exist, to the extent that a common fund of stories and legends associating the punitive dead man, the young hero, and inconstancy may have been a source for the theme taken up in Tirso de Molina's play. According to Rousset, more than 250 oral versions have been collected, in addition to innumerable written versions, for the sixteenth and seventeenth centuries alone. We must therefore separate the comedy from the myth that it puts on stage. Even if his mythic origins remain obscure, the figure of Don Juan predates Tirso de Molina's *Trickster*. Beyond the theatrical twists and turns that present it without having created it, the thesis of a modern myth brings Don Juan into connection with Faust, since a comparable analysis of the latter leads to the same conclusion.

Music (tonal music, at any rate) has no monopoly on variations on a theme. Structuralism, as applied to myth, speaks of the logic in which later developments depend on an initially determined framework. The theme is apparent behind each of the variations, even if it is masked by them. A relatively simple matrix can thus give rise to sophisticated constructs embodying the original idea and departing from it only to return to it all the more effectively through modulations. It is entirely possible to read Don Juan through this lens and to discern an established structure with a great many artistic or poetic variations that constantly maintain the structure without ever affirming it outright. Maurice Molho (1995) has separated out its constitutive units according to the method devised by Lévi-Strauss. Some elements turn out to be altogether secondary, as, for example, the existence of a valet, while others, like the statue of the Commandant, are essential to the "mythic structure." Inside the story itself, many variations can occur without challenging its underlying nature. Thus, for example, it is of secondary importance that Elvira left the convent to marry Don Juan or that she was abandoned by him. The group of women is itself subject to numerous fluctuations, from Tirso de Molina to Montherlant. The means employed by Don Juan in his seductions are hardly significant, while the power of the Eros that he incarnates is decisive when it comes to myth. Indeed, the moral law is never effective against the raging passions of Eros. Neither the rage of the Commandant nor the reprimands of the father (Molière), nor the admonitions of the king (Tirso de Molina), nor the reproaches of Elvira (Molière, Da Ponte/ Mozart), nor the cry for vengeance of Don Ottavio (Da Ponte/ Mozart), nor the threats of Don Carlos and Don Alonso (Molière), nor the warnings of the valet (whether he is named Catalinón, Sganarelle, or Leporello) have any effect whatsoever on Don Juan. Nothing can defeat Don Juan except a supernatural force, since he himself belongs to a realm beyond the natural. It comes as no surprise, therefore, that the sole victory of the moral order comes from heaven.

Because he relates no origin or founding murder and can hardly be said to mark the stages of an evolution in which rational thought would supplant magical thought, Don Juan can thus claim the status of myth, if we judge him by the yardstick of the science of myth that is structuralism. Fine. But then, what more do we know? This tells us nothing about how to make use of him, nor how this figure might perhaps help us understand why he remains so current.

Let us assume for a moment that we are dealing with an original myth. Georges Dumézil (1977), the natural father of structuralism who stopped using the term *structure* when ethnology started using it everywhere, came to believe that myths do not directly reflect the social organization that gave rise to them. As a historian, he tried to follow the incarnations of a myth from the time of its birth. In contrast to Lévi-Strauss, who was fascinated by the possible combinatories of the human mind and had little interest in the social and historical conditions that gave rise to myths, Dumézil attributes their creation to a powerful mental activity, to be sure, but one without any direct, simple relation to the underlying social structures. The case of Don Juan, then, calls for prudence. Although it is conceivable to analyze the theatrical representations of this figure in the wake of structuralism, and also possible to seek in the history of the Western imagination the matrix of the seducer, deciphering the result remains a delicate matter. Don Juan speaks to us, but we still have to wonder about the meaning of his words.

I have suggested that an additive approach to this enigmatic figure just causes confusion. It presupposes the enumeration of moral and physical characteristics so as to draw a portrait, with the major obstacle that the picture will vary greatly according to the time period and the chosen perspective. The Baroque seducer from the beginning of the seventeenth century yields to the classical libertine at its end, then to the defeated aristocrat of the eighteenth century and the tragic and romantic hero of the nineteenth. He returns in the twentieth as a desperate, aging Romeo overtaken by his own history. The twenty-first century may be getting ready to confirm the ideas of Joseph Delteil, going back to 1930, in which Don Juan is above all a prisoner of his attractiveness to women. Isn't he merely the slave of every female he meets?[1] Each age constructs its own Don Juan and projects a part of itself onto him. Tirso de Molina's great lord has little in common with the *Monsieur Jean* of Edouard Vaillant (1959). How can we orient ourselves amid all these changes?

In contrast, a subtractive approach consists in seeking what Don Juan is not. Here we have to cut back to the point where the implicit image dissolves, vanishes in a mist that surrounds it and blurs its contours. When this point is reached, when this threshold is crossed, a new perception of the figure comes into view. Instead of adding to the traditional imagery, we move away from all representation. This is how we arrive at the notion of a *conceptual figure*.

This expression is borrowed from Gilles Deleuze and Félix Guattari (1991), who use it to characterize a notion of Kierkegaard's. It refers to the process of becoming, or the subject, of a philosophy. Because he embodies a thought, a conceptual figure is radically different from an aesthetic figure or a psychosocial type. This is exactly what Kierkegaard (1846) maintains in contrasting Don Juan to Faust: "Faust is idea, but an idea that is also essentially an individual. To conceive of the spiritual-demonic concentrated in one individual is natural to thought, whereas to conceive of the sensuous in one individual is impossible. Don Juan

---

1. Thus Jean-Pierre Winter (1998) asks whether there is any woman in the world to whom Don Juan is able to say no.

continually hovers between being an idea—that is power, life—and being an individual" (p. 92).

Here we have the distinction between conceptual figure and psychosocial type. The former takes on a human form in order to incarnate a movement, an idea, a power; the latter is an individual who stands for a multitude. The conceptual figure is an anthropomorphic idea. The psychosocial type models a statistical summary. Don Juan oscillates between the two, because he can't be reduced to some individual or other, nor, at the same time, can he remain a mere abstraction. When it comes to Don Juan, our mind wavers between poetry, which creates images, and the demands of thought, which supplies concepts. This intermediate state appears under the composite aspect of a formed concept, by means of which thought becomes humanoid but refuses to reduce a social movement or collective development to a particular individual. A psychosocial type represents, condenses, summarizes. A conceptual figure is based on a human form so as to expand, open, sustain the imagination. The conceptual figure enables thought to unfold simultaneously in the world of abstraction and the world of the everyday. A proper noun from a historical perspective, "Don Juan" has thus become a common noun from a logical perspective. And we need both in order to think.

But it would be an error to set up a firm contrast between psychosocial type and conceptual figure. Though not the same, they are closely related to one another. The oscillation of which Kierkegaard speaks in regard to Don Juan is true of Faust as well, as for Tristan or Sisyphus. But whereas in some cases it tends toward the aesthetic figure (Faust and Tristan), in others it inclines toward the concept (Don Juan and Sisyphus). A character in a novel (Rastignac, Rogogine, Bovary, Drogo, among many others) does not condense in his or her "person" the complex lines of individual and social evolution. Yet he or she can lend physical features to the conceptual figure. Thus we have seen Don Juan dressed up in the body of Miguel de Mañara, and even, some say, in that of Louis XIV or the Duke of Lauzun! But if Don Juan is actually a conceptual figure, his physical appearance cannot be confined to any sort of aesthetic image. To take another example, if each of us feels the need for a symbolic death, and if we go through the painful stages of a kind of transfiguration—psychological, to be sure, but perhaps also physical—like that of Gregor Samsa in Kafka's *Metamorphosis*, and if this adventure sums up the drama of the human condition in the twentieth century, then Kafka's hero may become a conceptual figure. He thus enables us to give shape to a thought; to represent in a human way a process of reasoning and becoming; to cheat a bit, somehow, so as to give life to the abstraction of the pure concept. But if Gregor Samsa remains the protagonist of a narrative, however fascinating, he falls into the category of psychosocial types and is of little use to us in thinking about the way we think about ourselves.

Approaching Don Juan as a conceptual figure makes his human appearance secondary and, in a word, anecdotal. Through him a pure force is expressed, and so the concrete details of putting it into practice seem less significant. It is probably an imprecision or a concession on Molière's part to show us in too much detail how the seducer goes about attracting women and achieving his ends. The extensive treatment of the hypocritical marriage promise misses its goal, since it turns against the women it is supposed to defend; depicting women as automatically succumbing to the prospect of marriage assumes a high degree of naiveté on their part. Even if the contractual union represents a social guarantee, to assume that sexual pleasure must lead to marriage subordinates the woman to the man who marries her, even before the wedding. She imprisons her body in the spirit of the times. In the course of three centuries, the evolution of lifestyle and of the collective conscience has refuted such a vision.

To express the idea that two people love one another, the Japanese say *aisuru*, which literally means "love to make." This apparently impersonal assertion deprives seduction of subjectivity and designates an attraction that cannot be reduced to wanting, even if the love object is implied. Here, two drives come together and give rise to pleasure. The French expression "to make love" follows the same logic. That's how it is with Don Juan: as soon as he appears, his charm sets to work. He doesn't have to promise marriage, or offer trinkets, or strut about. If he spends time on such trickery, it is only for the fun of it or for purely aesthetic reasons, since he has won the game even before it begins. He doesn't seduce women because he has an infallible gimmick like a magician, but because a pure force of seduction is expressed through him. He is the sensual attractor par excellence. All he has to do is show up, and seduction is there. It is also possible, however, to reverse the proposition without changing its essential nature: as soon as a woman comes on the scene, Don Juan succumbs. This amounts to saying that charm arises from the joint presence of the protagonists and is not attached to one or the other pole of the relation. Still, there is only one Don Juan and a myriad of women, and therein lies the fundamental inequality of the "couple" comprising a male seducer and seductive females. All by himself, Don Juan already incarnates an asymmetry.

Listen to Mozart's *Don Giovanni*, Kierkegaard tells us, and if that does not give you an idea of this figure, you will never have one.[2] For this philosopher, only music can convey an idea of his profound nature, the embodiment of an erotic force in action. Through his own movement Don Juan gives life to the other characters and their passions, and this is why Mozart's opera conveys this impression. Music allows for the simultaneous development of several ideas that reveal the richness of feelings and the ambiguity of behaviors. It expresses the contradictions that discourse would have to set forth in a linear, and thus reductive, fashion. Writing flattens. Music sculpts. Its unfolding combines the verticality of harmony with the horizontality of melody and in this way makes possible the most complex intertwinings.

Don Giovanni presents a series of reversals. Don Juan fails in his attempt with regard to Anna and is forced to

---

2. Kierkegaard is exaggerating a bit. The last part of Glück's ballet also offers a striking musical approach to Don Juan.

flee the Commandant's palace. When caught, he kills the man, though not without having tried to avoid this senseless murder. He commits it, as it were, in spite of himself. Killing was not in his plans; it is just an unforeseen consequence of acts undertaken in pursuit of his irrepressible desire. Now here he is seducing Zerlina, but he does not achieve his goal, since Elvira takes the peasant girl away. Two failures, then. It is as though Don Juan can succeed only with Death, who, herself seduced in a certain sense, will go all the way. Don Juan swallowed up in the entrails of the earth: Isn't this a symbol of the greatest love? Between the defeat in Anna's room and his death during the banquet in honor of the Commandant, very little time elapses. *Don Giovanni* presents the final day of Don Juan. And the very fact that nothing happens in the way of real seduction, but only failures and lists enumerating past exploits, is enough to prove that the means employed by the hero are of no great importance. A force passes through Don Juan, and although it has taken on his form it can never be reduced to it.[3] Mozart attributes to Don Juan this force in motion. He imposes it like an idea in action, and the title role is no longer just an individual, even if, according to the memoirs of Lorenzo da Ponte, this result was not the librettist's main concern.

---

3. During a radio broadcast on October 10, 1998, the conductor Ricardo Muti related how, after the dress rehearsal of a *Don Giovanni* that he had led in the staging of Giorgio Strehler, the latter had said to him, "We thought we showed Don Giovanni, but we didn't succeed." Strehler started walking away and then turned back to Muti, adding with passion, "And no one ever will."

As an individual who does not try to hide his true nature, Don Juan is certainly of interest, especially for the contradictory feelings of repulsion and attraction that he inspires. Doesn't a cad who admits to being a cad at least compel a certain sympathy? Without absolving him, we can give him consideration. But this interest remains limited. In general, the biographies of seducers are as boring as they can be, except for Casanova's, which goes far beyond the usual man–woman account and places its author among the most brilliant and enlightened minds of the eighteenth century. As Idea, on the other hand, Don Juan symbolizes pure sensuality. This exceptional dimension calls for a thorough account of the dross associated with him. An image of a great lord, beautifully dressed and loaded with wealth and property, would interfere with our understanding of his universality.

The notion of a conceptual figure allows for oscillation between two poles. On the one hand, no concept has ever made love with a woman; on the other, the idea of Don Juan that we construct for ourselves eludes the definitive grasp of thought. One minute we imagine him as a man busily going about seduction, the next minute we catch ourselves and, with a wry smile, realize that no one can love a thousand and three women—and that just in Spain. While we are pausing at this latter determination, Don Juan reclaims his rights in our imagination, and once again we let ourselves be swept along in his inexorable course.

Don Juan is thus the opposite of a unity. Faithful to his rule, but a man of words without speech. Deprived of a given name, but given a name known by all. Unknowable because always hidden, but universally recognizable because always masked. A fugitive, but brave. A tireless seducer, but unfailingly seduced before he seduces. An inveterate liar, but sincere in the moment. Acknowledging his debts, but never paying them. Unfailingly merry, but a friend of death. Certain of the justice of his life that is nevertheless a life of uncertainty. Occasionally a murderer, but valiant if necessary. Powerful like a great lord, but without possessions like a beggar. A hypocrite in his spare time, but playing the hypocrite in order to have fun with hypocrisy. A man with aims but without projects. Plural and for that very reason truly singular, Don Juan is thus the unity of opposites.

This last trait is a general characteristic of the mythic hero, the one whose story offers a solution to the primary conflicts experienced by the members of a society. The contradictions of his culture find a solution in him and through him. In this way, he gives form to the desire of the individual who is incapable of violating social prohibitions. In *Man and the Sacred*, Roger Caillois (1938) suggests that the grandeur proper to myth does not absolve the hero of guilt but rather authorizes it. The guilty hero substitutes for the ordinary individual and realizes the impossible. As for ritual, it enables the individual to take part in heroic actions.

Don Juan has all the features of the hero when observed from the outside, as it were, but as soon as we hear him speak through his multiple representations—theatrical, poetic, musical, and others—he is devoid of all heroism, until finally, in the twentieth century, he states this himself. If the garments of the hero fit him badly, do we dare view him as a mere fantasy of the West? That would not be enough to exhaust the modern dimension of this figure. His obsession is not limited to sex (beneath the libertine is the pervert, Foucault says). He has within him a vital urgency that makes it possible for him to accomplish what the rest of us cannot reach. He resolves the major contradiction between the permanent and the momentary, between balance and openness.

Some authors, as we have seen, judge him according to the women he wins. A male whore, a plaything in feminine hands, a liberator: Tirso de Molina himself calls him "women's punishment." A fantasy in the feminine gender, then? That would be a bit too simple, first because Don Juan tends to reduce every woman to flesh and to be interested only in her body, despite the efforts of some writers to exonerate him in this regard, and then because the feminine gaze is rare among authors attached to this figure. Don Juan remains a creature of the male imagination and, in the worst cases, one who encourages their most primal urges and those alone. And, finally, because such a fantasy would transform women into principal agents of individual emancipation, which is something that the story does not confirm.

As a conceptual figure, Don Juan embodies a process of liberation that affects women and men alike. This process is related to the emergence of a new force: the individual. In its ceaseless agitation, it finally upsets the social order and established values. Thus, as a conceptual figure, this strange hero certainly tells us something about something, to use Ricoeur's formula, but precisely what about what?

In his relations with women, with money, and with God, Don Juan constantly foils the logic of symmetrical reciprocity. In so doing, he presents a remarkable case of ruptures.

PART II

RUPTURES

FOUR

DISPOSSESSION

In the society in which Don Juan shines darkly like a comet, possessions make the man. The nobleman possesses land and servants, the bourgeois goods and money. That the former is learning to concede defeat in the face of the advances of the latter will have no effect on the dominant economic arrangement. For a long time to come, patrimonial accumulation will remain an obvious sign of wealth. Beyond the various aspects of ownership and the customs proper to the classes and estates of society, one continuous motif is apparent: possessing, heaping up, amassing.

We have no reliable information about the patrimony attributed to Don Juan. A great lord but penniless, he has everything he wants and multiplies debts. With regard to the goods of this world, he is in the position of a naked king: he possesses nothing but has everything at his disposal. He is thus the opposite of a pauper or a rich man. As usual, he escapes any categorization. And not only does he have nothing, he is nothing. It is not that he lacks substance, but, as Camus (1942) puts it, he chose to be nothing. This choice will enable him to find pleasure.

To possess is to keep. But Don Juan's logic belongs to another order. He scorns acquisition, needs movement, speed, play. He does not possess, he obtains. The Latin *obtinere* means to occupy, to maintain. It conveys the idea of taking hold, not of holding on. To obtain is to exercise one's influence with the aim not of acquisition or possession but of jubilation. This defines Don Juan's general attitude toward both property and women. Thus he does not "take" them, except in the sexual sense of the term. He merely exercises influence over them and vice versa. Why would he need possessions, since he quite naturally has women at his disposal like property? He who possesses is possessed, writes Nietzsche (1886). Don Juan dispossesses himself of what might possess him, so as to attain a state of complete pleasure.

He renounces the patrimony. Though he is poor in Molière's sense, this is of no concern to him, strong as he is in his power of indebtedness. When it comes to women, he acts as though he were calmly exercising a right. In contrast to someone like Almaviva, conquered by the Revolution, he has nothing to fear from any social upheaval, since he himself is a kind of permanent revolution. In contrast to the thirst for patrimony that gradually permeates societies in which capitalism is spreading, and with it the emphasis on quantity, Don Juan knows that property leads nowhere. Goods imprison their master in slavery, and he has contempt for voluntary servitude.

If he possesses women, in what sense, then, are we to understand this? Does he collect them? Does he deceive them? Does the seducer always carry around a little pad in which to write the names of his conquests? Does he, in addition, have the bad taste to make notes at each entry?

The idea of a list of women one has seduced is a very old one in the literary tradition, even if it is expressed differently in different periods. In the sixteenth and seventeenth centuries, Seville was considered "universal." To win the favors of Sevillian women was highly significant. In the *Trickster*, Don Juan courts and seduces as many plebeians (Tisbea and Aminta) as aristocrats (Isabela and Ana). In Mozart, the famous "catalogue" aria announces the unthinkable: "In Italy, six hundred and forty; in Germany, two hundred and one, a hundred in France; in Turkey ninety-one; but . . . but, in Spain, there are already a thousand and three!" The inventory (totaling two thousand thirty-five here) certainly seems like a collection.

But let us be wary of hasty conclusions. Does it make sense to imagine Don Juan armed with his notebook, writing down each conquest? What good would that do him? Would he read over the list, each evening at the fireside, before going to sleep? Would he re-experience pursuits and captures by going over the names on the list? Would he compare the virtues of each of his victims? Would he boast once again in the presence of his friends (though he has none) or his valet? In old age, would he reread the list nostalgically, recalling the high points of his youth?

These hypotheses make no sense. Don Juan has no interest in making a list of conquests. He gets what he wants, takes his pleasure, gives pleasure, and goes on his way. He scores a victory and could not care less about putting it down on paper. He has never made any list of his female adventures. What does Leporello tell us? "Madamina, this is the catalogue of the beautiful women my master loved— I myself made it"* ("*Madamina, il catologo è questo / Delle belle che amò il padron mio, / Un catologo egli è che ho fatto io*"). "I myself made it": the catalogue is thus the work not of the master but of his manservant. While the seducer thinks only of his pleasure, his servant keeps a list. Don Juan never stops but goes ahead in pursuit of pleasure to come. To stay in one place is to risk danger. But Leporello always has a time lag, and the catalogue reveals the gap that separates the two figures. One moves, the other stops. One is possessed by his desire for women but intentionally dispossessed, the other is a possessor deprived of possession. Because Don Juan possesses nothing, nothing stops him. Because Leporello is a possessor, everything holds him back. Don Juan loves. Leporello keeps count. Do we enumerate the passing days when we set out to attack life?

Imagining that possession satisfies desire is like thinking you can put out fire with straw. Don Juan catches fire and follows his path inexorably, without turning back. Through the catalogue, however, the manservant tries to tell his master's story. This logic of summation will never achieve its goal: Don Juan has no story, just innumerable stories that leave no trace in his memory. Leporello, fascinated by what he thinks of as essentially a technique, uses the menu to tell Elvira about his master's strategy, the attractions of which he details with a certain poor taste.

---

*All unattributed translations are by S. F.

Doesn't he actually emphasize the aim of everything the seducer has been accused of? The last sentence of his monologue, "*Voi sapete quel che fa!*" ("You know what he does!"), is even sung to a tune that follows the rhythm of the final stages of the sex act. Mozart arranged his music to correspond to foreplay, penetration, and the explosion of orgasm, all with strength and gentleness. Before Wagner's overture to *Tristan und Isolde*, in which we hear the slow increase and then the detumescence of masculine desire, Mozart expresses what the theater cannot show or speech say without risking pornography. But it is Leporello who is telling the story, in his master's absence. Don Juan is already far away from this moment in which he is spoken of.

If there is a correspondence between what one might call individual markers and the lines of force of a culture, it is surely no accident that Don Juan first appears in Seville. Spain gives rise to a figure who is constantly moving, stirring, agitating in order to survive. For centuries, France has been a country in which one comes to rest, in which invaders from the North and the East finally settle down, the country to which people come to taste the sweetness of life (there is even a German saying, "happy as God in France"). In contrast, Spain is first of all a place of turbulence, of departures, escapes, collisions. People are glad to establish themselves in France. In the Iberian peninsula, people become impassioned. A land of battles and brutal contrasts, Spain offered America to Europe and formed a barrier against Islam. A culture in which death and life are intertwined like lovers, it was at the same time the cradle of two *enfants terribles* of the Western imagination, both transgressors of law and custom: Don Juan and Don Quixote. In very different ways, both of them stigmatize modernity as it arises. The latter mocks it, while the former denies its foundations—or is it the reverse?

Like his country of origin, Don Juan is primarily a man of contrasts and encounters, always transient. His marriage with Elvira was a failure, not in the sense of an unsuccessful union but because the "marrier of the human race" actually had to yield in order to win the favors of this woman. For Don Juan, a kept promise is a defeat. A man of encounters, to be sure, but not a man of connections. Always in pursuit, he can't stay still for an instant. How can we imagine him married? On the contrary, he is always in flight, only this is not the stealing away of a fugitive but a mariner's strategy. Flight makes it possible to reef in when the wind grows stronger. This attitude takes one far from familiar horizons and leads to the discovery of unknown lands. It enables Don Juan to follow the most unexpected paths and to lose himself in order better to save himself. Don't two meanings coexist in this last verb: to escape a danger and to assure one's survival? Don Juan saves himself in one sense in order to save himself in the other. In so doing, he outstrips his detractors as well as his pursuers.

For him, the unknown is a noun of feminine gender and preferably a plural one. He finds his way out only in these unknown beings. Thus Molière compares him to Alexander the Great: "There is nothing that can halt the impetuousness of my desires, I feel in me a heart that can love the whole earth; and, like Alexander, I would wish there were

other worlds, so that I could extend my amorous conquests."
This analogy with the famous conqueror is of twofold
interest. First, Alexander was never vanquished. Setting
out in 334 B.C., he reached the basin of the Indus eight
years later, having overcome Syria, Phoenicia, Egypt, Meso-
potamia, the Persian Empire, and Afghanistan. But, one
day in July, 326, his armies refused to go any further. Where,
then, did Alexander intend to go? Wasn't he following a
road within himself, and weren't his various conquests just
the stages, relays, results of an endless march? Wasn't the
aim of this matchless conqueror's work simply to work, as
Montaigne reminds us? In any case, he agreed to turn back
after having subdued Asia. Had he had at his disposal soldiers of his caliber, he might have proved that the earth is
round! The second point of comparison is that the figure
of Don Juan is like that of a warrior. The warrior's victories are never an end in themselves but moments on the
road that unfailingly leads him to death. The warrior fights
primarily in order to fight. Don Juan conquers in order to
conquer.

Leporello's catalogue draws up a balance sheet. But
nothing could be further from his master than accountancy.
Why would he go in for it? What good would it do him to
count up his victories, since his arithmetic has nothing in
common with Euclid's? When his valet asks him what he
believes, Don Juan answers exactly the way the Prince of
Nassau confessed to a theologian an hour before his death,
if we are to believe Tallemant des Réaux (1653), that two
and two make four and four and four make eight. Such
realism frees our man from any other morality. But his acts

give the lie to this belief in a logic. The greater the number of conquered women, the less each one counts. More precisely, Don Juan sets down the terms of an original and complex arithmetic. Instead of a simple addition, $1 + 1 = 2$, he invents an operation of the type $1 + 1 = 0$, that is, $1 = -1$! Each additional woman erases the preceding ones. In Molière, Don Juan has hardly escaped the rage of Elvire, and the equally terrible fury of the waves, when he meets Charlotte and immediately starts courting her. He chases, in two complementary senses of the verb: pursue and dismiss. He chases one woman, and one woman chases away another. Each new conquest abolishes the prior ones. They do not add up, as imagined by his "victims," his critics, or those who envy him, but instead cancel each other out, vanishing as they accumulate. In Leporello's catalogue, women are added one to the other. This is a logic of summation. But Don Juan subtracts, in all the senses of the term: he robs men of their power, takes their women, and, as a crowning touch, erases one conquest with the next. For Da Ponte/ Mozart, when he is after a new pleasure he catches a whiff of a feminine presence ("*Mi pare sentir odor di femmina*"). It will turn out that this woman is none other than Elvira! Thus a woman can cancel herself out. And so, to the odd arithmetic we have already noted, we can add a new operatory rule: $1 = 0$.

Such an arithmetic is socially inappropriate. For the rest of the world, addition adds. For Don Juan, it destroys. If he marries women, this means solely that his body is punctually conjoined with theirs. Clearly, he cannot possess them; this patrimonial relation is entirely foreign to him. Must we conclude that he betrays them all? Can he possess only in the sense of deceiving? But what would deceiving mean, then? Making love with an "irregular," not keeping his word, acting in opposition to his words?

A hasty examination of Don Juan's relation to women can lead us astray. From the outset, he passes for a cad or a vulgar consumer, "a monster, traitor, the depths of deceit," in Elvira's abusive terms according to Da Ponte. A charmer, a hoaxer, he never stops deceiving. He makes commitments but forgets them immediately. He makes promises, but only to go back on them at the first opportunity. Women, in this view, are nothing but a "large herd of sacrificial victims," to use Baudelaire's phrase.

Isn't such an attitude evidence of a real contempt for women? To see and to love, just love: Is that contempt? Is this figure's sensuality, entirely physical, an affront to women as people? Are we to reproach Don Juan with being interested only in bodies, in all shapes and sizes without exception, as Leporello is eager to explain ("They include country women, chambermaids, city women, countesses, baronesses, marquises, princesses, women of all ranks, sizes, ages")? Since no woman escapes Don Juan's desire, at least there can be no question of blaming his taste. He is not looking for Woman—which would presuppose an ideal, and he has none—but rather the pleasure of the flesh, which is attained only through women.[1] His sensual power

---

1. In contrast, Cherubino in *The Marriage of Figaro* has no objections to masturbation if feminine love is not available: "*E se non ho chi m'oda,/ Parlo d'amor con me*" ("If I have no one to hear me, I speak of love to myself").

49

is satisfied only with them. From his perspective, women are not victims, animals, prey, or even objects, but necessary complements. Born imperfect, incomplete, Don Juan is nothing without women. He exists through them. If you do away with them, he vanishes. The motive may be different from what one might think. Could it be that woman is propulsion, the force of the drive?

However, as we have seen, in *Don Giovanni* we witness a series of failed seductions. Don Juan was unable to win Anna's favors, Elvira keeps on trying to unmask him, Zerlina finally escapes him. And yet his erotic power is not undermined in the least. He pursues his quest. The reversals are just the sign of a bad day—a very bad day, in fact his last, since he will encounter the Commandant and continue his errand in hell. In other words, the lack of a woman does not at all put an end to Don Juan's appetite. The possible existence of a woman to be conquered is all he needs to justify his own existence. Women are his permanent feast. And, moreover, how could we imagine them lacking, since they too are traversed by desire that must be slaked?

If the representation of the male, in this vision, is far from brilliant, what shall we say about the seduced women? The impostor appears, and they succumb. The desire embodied by the seducer thus overcomes any resistance. If we look at Don Juan's erotic potency in a mirror, don't we see the blaze of female passion? If Don Juan tries to make love to every woman he passes, don't we have to conclude that all women instantaneously exercise their power of seduction over him? Does attraction work in only one direction?

In the Spain of Don Juan's birth, the subordination of women borders on total dependence, not only from the economic point of view but also from the sexual one. So much so that a woman's violated virginity is never her concern but the concern of her father or brothers. For Molière, Don Carlos and Don Alonse look for Don Juan in order to avenge their sister, Elvire, whom he took from the convent, married, and abandoned. Their duty is to restore the family's tarnished honor. All of Elvire's interventions, however, show only the sincerity of a disappointed woman torn between her loving feelings and her horror at the behavior of a man she is still taken with. She does not reproach her lover and husband with having led her to break her sacred vows. Removed from the convent with her consent, loved physically, here too with her consent, Elvire assumes her new condition of abandoned woman but does not cry out her despair at having been snatched from divine love to be initiated into the human variety. It is easy to imagine that she followed Don Juan because he released her from a life dedicated to abstinence and prayer, offering her the discovery of human love to boot. In her remonstrations, Elvire is still trying to look for ways to excuse Don Juan's behavior and never calls into question her adventure with him. When she accidentally meets him as he is getting a new maneuver underway, she tells him the arguments he should have employed instead of remaining dumbfounded and unable to respond. At the end of her indictment she switches to the familiar form of address, a sign of renewed closeness, and adds that, if heaven holds no fear for him, he should at least fear the wrath of an offended woman. This is, therefore, a matter between a man and a woman, between two human beings on the same level. Elvire understands that Don Juan believes in neither heaven nor hell, and she situates herself accordingly. She speaks to him as a woman who has become responsible for her life and her fate. In the same way, the Elvira of Da Ponte/ Mozart, who has no family, asks no one to avenge her. Her pain is related to her abandonment, her betrayal, not to the fact of having succumbed. Nothing in what she says suggests that she regrets anything. She, too, laments the end of their relationship, not its nature.

In both cases, clearly, Elvire/ Elvira acts like a scorned, wounded, bruised woman, but first and foremost as simply a woman and not a tool of her family. She never complains of dishonor. Coming to terms with her actions, she shifts the general and societal question of the honor of name and family to a concern on the individual level. She, and no one else, is involved. Ultimately, she expects nothing from anyone, not even from heaven.

Do we have here a basis for a view of Don Juan as a liberator of women? Perhaps so, but was it ever an intention of Don Juan's to be a liberator? He is guided not by a wish but by an unquenchable thirst. Let others follow their own path; as for him, he is a free man. If Elvira has left the convent, made love with him, let herself be deceived by promises he made on the spur of the moment in order to seduce her, whom can she blame? An immoral morality, you say? Certainly. But Don Juan has no use for morality. Each time he makes a commitment he is sincere, because he exists only in the moment. The only thing that counts for him is the gratification of a desire that, once gratified, finds that it needs gratification. Don Juan acutely experiences this twofold constraint without ever being able to get beyond it. If he gets what he wants, he is happy, but as soon as he has gotten it he becomes unhappy. Hence his intermittent sincerity and global infidelity, because a series of sincerities do not add up to fidelity. In contrast to Mérimée's Carmen, Don Juan does not lie. He tells the truth each time but always contradicts himself. Added end to end, these partial truths amount to a continuous lie. More precisely, everything depends on the perspective one adopts.

When a skeptical Leporello asks him at the beginning of Act II of *Don Giovanni* whether he is brave enough to deceive all women, the seducer ingenuously replies that, if he were faithful to one woman, he would be cruel to the others; only those who do not understand him think he is a betrayer. And indeed, he is always making commitments, since this is his mode of being. He always acts in the register of beginning and not that of repetition (cf. Kofman and Masson 1991). A devotee of the eternally new beginning, he repeats only by starting over again. This explains why he heeds no warnings and remains undisturbed. And it no doubt also explains why we can't get free of the strange feeling that Don Juan is playing with his life. He seems to flee death and seek it at the same time. This is quite clear in Montherlant, but also in all the other great authors, especially Tirso de Molina, Da Ponte/ Mozart, or Molière. Events move forward as though an implacable destiny were at work in the wings. Curiously, Don Juan keeps on throwing himself in the path of his pursuers: this is one of the meanings of the presence of the Commandant, whether in the flesh or in stone. From his first appearance, Don Juan's fate is sealed, as is so well suggested by Mozart's initial chords.[2] Beginning again, up to the end, toward and against everything, is what leads Don Juan to keep on making commitments.

With women first of all, of course, but he also makes promises right and left to his various creditors. Promising is his relation to the other. But where every other man gives his word in anticipation of future actions, he merely commits himself, and that is all. In contrast to the knight's, his word carries no obligation. In fact, Don Juan does not engage himself, he engages. In this sense, he is a man of initiatives, as Blanchot (1969) says. His engagements are the beginnings of a match or the initial passes of a fight. "When I make a promise, I . . . make a promise" could be his motto.

His engagement where women are concerned is thus never a matrimonial, let alone patrimonial, one. In the capitalist effervescence of the seventeenth century, a new configuration of the world was being established. The traditional methods of appropriating the goods of others

---

2. We know for certain that Mozart composed the Overture to *Don Giovanni* during the night preceding the first performance of the opera on October 20, 1787. The initial motif announces the atmosphere of the entire work right from the start. The first notes are marked by the stamp of the Commandant, and this motif recurs in Scene V of the second act, when the statue of the Commandant breaks forth. The orchestration of these passages is almost religious: additional evidence for Mozart's exactness, since, in the Spain of Alfonso XI (where the drama is supposed to take place), a Commandant in a military order is a priest and a warrior, a soldier-monk.

(plundering, raiding, subjugation) were being supplanted by a concern for production. The burying of treasure, the growing shortage of booty, the improvement of defensive techniques, and the rising cost of waging war gradually led princes to turn to the riches of their own territory instead of attempting capture elsewhere.

In the pursuit of fortune, production comes to take the place of warfare. An entire social arrangement is put in place, one in which historians see a decisive shift opening out onto modernity (cf. Duby 1973). At the same time that the other stops being one's prey, his property becomes a possession that one can draw to oneself in nonbellicose ways. One very old method comes to assist production (though production is accorded priority), and this is alliance. In joining with the other, one can enlarge one's wealth without bloodshed. In this context, marriage is a trump card of captation. Whatever the contractual specifications, it contributes to the increase and transmission of a family's property. Although love may be a factor, marriage is first and foremost an economic agreement. Among princes, it ensures peace or allows the avoidance of war, and in so doing it serves a vital function at a time when warfare was becoming costly. And so it absolutely had to be protected against anything that might attack it.

Before the Council of Trent (1545–1563), all a man and a woman had to do was exchange secret vows in order to establish a religious union. The betrothed couple (this traditional term speaks for itself) had no need of authorizations or official declarations, nor of a contract. The Council would change everything. Essentially devoted to the precise definition of dogma and to the reorganization of the discipline of the Catholic orders, it also dealt with marriage. Its influence, which was considerable, radically altered the situation of the spouses by suppressing the freedom of marital alliance. It reinforced parental authority and emphasized the importance of priests. A marriage was now valid only with the approval of a man of the Church and after publication of the banns. With these new rules, the transmission of property would be more controllable by the family and also by the state, which was, of course, of a deeply religious nature.

Is morality lacking in all of this development? Probably not, but marriage is too important an economic issue to be reduced to love. And, though Jean-Jacques Rousseau, two centuries later, thought that marital love was the model of a heavenly life, the Council of Trent was hardly interested in heaven. Even if self-righteous morality was given its due, it was not love that was promoted but above all the transmission of property and the continuation of lineages, while affirming the supremacy of the Church over the monarchy.

It remains the case that both kinds of marriage, pre- and post-Tridentine, leave the woman vulnerable to being possessed, in the two senses of the term. In the first case, she can easily be abused; in the second, she becomes merely a reproducer and purveyor of property (cf. Molho 1995). As for Don Juan, he behaves the same before and after the Council of Trent: *Voi sapete quel che fa* ("You know what he does").

In a society in which human relations are determined by Nature, and in which social status derives from an exteriority whose basis is never questioned but is accepted once and for all, interpersonal dealings have nothing to do with decisions freely arrived at but instead with codes established a priori. Sociologists call this type of situation one of communal ties. It is as though the structure of society were granted to men by a divinity external to their lives. A supernatural power defines the social surround, and no one can challenge this framework without infringing on the will of heaven. This architecture is gradually replaced with a radically different organization based on contractual relations. The new dispensation took a long time to prevail, and, a hundred years before the French Revolution, the charter signed by William III of England at the end of the seventeenth century ratified the fundamental importance of the contract as a mode of relation between individuals. This was not the case in the Middle Ages, nor even at the beginning of sixteenth-century Europe. The feudal imagination, as Jacques Le Goff calls it, forbids any emergence of the notion of a contract separate from interpersonal ties.

It is in this context that Don Juan makes commitments without ever respecting them. At a time when society is slowly discovering the meaning of a relation formed on the basis of contractual reciprocity, he disturbs the balance. In fact, he refuses any obligation. Neither the constriction of communal order nor the reciprocity of contractual order suits him. Right from the outset, he situates himself on the margin of any social project.

Tirso de Molina had scarcely presented the divine punishment overwhelming Don Juan when the latter freed himself from his creator and achieved a disturbing independence. In the *Trickster*, the society of men with their God of vengeance denies Don Juan the absolution that he calls for *in extremis*. From the eighteenth century on, however, through an exchange of roles between this figure and the rest of society, it is he who majestically scorns the divine forgiveness for which everyone urges him to beg.

In the first configuration, the individual does not assert himself in the face of society. He remains one of the wheels of a vast mechanism whose architecture is to be found in heaven as well as on earth, and whose order includes God and men. God created Nature, and the power of the monarch derives from God as a matter of course. Nature, governed by the Almighty, assigns society its organization. It is thus "natural" that the prince is placed above the people, as though between earth and heaven. It is also "natural" that immutable and transcendent laws determine good and evil, and, finally, it is "natural" that the individual (a concept that became prevalent only gradually and quite belatedly in history a few centuries ago) is just one element of this extraordinary clockwork, as Voltaire called it.

In the second configuration, everything is inverted. The notion of the individual is affirmed, and a personal will can succeed in changing the world. Human history no longer flows from a principle external to humanity. On the contrary, the fuel for the human motor is found on earth. The divine will retreats before the nose of Cleopatra, which all by itself could alter the face of the world. The determinants of action lie in the heart of the person who carries it out. Man governs himself, becoming his own master and the master of the entire universe. The Cartesian *cogito* stands as the defense of this very idea. Do we have to be reminded that the *Discourse on Method* was published in Leiden in 1637, that is, seven years after the first known edition of Molina's *Trickster?* Cartesian subjectivity, of course, did not arise from nowhere; little by little, the idea of individual freedom was gaining ground in the whole of society. From the seventeenth century on, it was possible to ascend in the social hierarchy through one's personal efforts. Though rare at the outset, the examples multiplied until, several centuries later, this became one of the fundamental ways of rising in society.

To be sure, the philosophical expression of subjectivity tends more to follow the enlargement of the power of the individual than to precede it, but this is of little importance. When Descartes pronounces his famous sentence, he is taking part in a general movement of thought based on the individual. The latter will gradually stop being a concept and will become a concrete body, free and independent. But it would be a long time before the impetus conveyed by Hobbes and McIntyre, and carried forward by the liberal theses of Hume, Locke, Mandeville, and Adam Smith, would lead to the recognition of the individual as the foundation of social theories.

The libertarian aspirations of Don Juan go so far that, like Napoleon, he can claim to have no ancestors. We have already looked at the role of the father in Tirso de Molina and Molière. It is significant that the later Don Juans, beginning with Mozart's, have no father. Not only do we never hear of Don Juan's mother, except for two or three vague allusions in Molière, but his father finally vanishes altogether. How better to show a person's independence? In contrast to modern man, of whom Freud (1939) speaks in *Moses and Monotheism*, and who resembles his predecessors so closely in his infantile wish for protection, Don Juan in no way seeks the support of a father, a man on earth or God in heaven. Orphaned and emancipated, he sums up the characteristics of the emerging free individual. This attitude involves no contempt, no superiority complex. Don Juan has no arrogance, no desperate pride, but a total presence of mind and body: he is at ease in the present, and too bad for the devout!

A great defender of his rights as an individual yet lacking a social project, Don Juan embodies the rising power of an unbridled subjectivity. He heightens individualistic tendencies to the point of turning them into a fratricidal struggle between the man he symbolizes and the society that witnesses his debauchery. The slaking of his desires brings him a transient gratification. If he abandons himself to a rampant individualism, the indignation of others places the only limit on his excesses. This represents a betrayal of the hope that Rabelais (1534) placed in his Abbey of Thélème. The famous rule inscribed at the beginning of the new moral and humanistic world, "Do as you will," is certainly one that Don Juan follows, but he is in no sense freely inclined to virtue, as are the people of whom Rabelais speaks, wellborn people who instinctively avoid vice (although, he reminds us, the human tendency is to undertake what is forbidden to us and covet what we are denied). Whereas the true Thélémites must be able to find within themselves the stability that will enable them to progress along the path of wisdom, Don Juan knows no inner limit, no counter-weight. In a world of hypocritical and harmful rules, closed off to pleasure and fenced in by economic requirements, he goes his own unique way. To the splendor of the plan of the Abbey of Thélème he opposes the simple demand for pleasure in life. And, from the outset, his individualism comes up against the social project that happens to be the most humanistic one there is.

Lacking ambition himself, Don Juan does not try to bring about the liberty of others. He does not fight for the coming of a society freed of its shackles, or for a conscience purified of everything that poisons it. Having no wish to change the world, he does not bother to change others. What matters most to him is to bring his actions into accord with his wishes, even if this complicates his thoughts and words a bit. This perhaps makes him the most remarkable desiring machine that the Western imagination has ever produced. His desires make women into transient goals or mere means. With them he travels only half of the road leading to individual freedom. The case of Elvire/ Elvira is emblematic here.

In Molière, Don Juan takes her from the convent, with her agreement, and marries her in the sense that he enjoys her body. As usual, he commits himself and then leaves. Elvire remains in love with her deceitful husband and doesn't condemn him strongly. Hadn't she consented? When she visits him, she asks him to mend his ways. Her words are inspired not so much by love felt at the moment as by homage to the love she used to feel for him. And she expects no reply from him. He simply asks her to stay; she refuses and departs. This is a first manifestation of her individuality as a woman. Don Juan did not free her as a person but only liberated her from societal bonds. His is the role not of a revolutionary trying to overturn society but of a free electron. It is only accidental that he helps to break the chains of the socially oppressed woman. Such a woman is dependent on her father or her brothers, who bear the responsibility for her honor. She remains a female body liable to being bargained over in anticipation of marriage. Do we have to be reminded that love and marriage were two different things in Christian theology? Not that marriage precludes love, but it in no way requires it. Denis de Rougemont (1970, Appendix 4) reports the Countess of Champagne as saying, in 1174, that love cannot extend its rights between husband and wife. Why? Because lovers give themselves to one another freely and mutually, while spouses are bound by duty to one another's will. (Hence the perennial conflict, in classical theater, between the girl who wants to marry her swain and the father who negotiates a contract for a good match.)

Don Juan explodes this fine arrangement in which the woman is an object of social transaction. And yet he offers nothing beside the undoing of an enslavement. He helps to free Elvira from her chains, but, once she is unchained, he offers her no means to assert control over her freedom. His only aim is to find pleasure, and her freedom is not a responsibility of his. Who else but Elvire herself could accomplish the second part of the journey? It is up to her to manage. Just as the society within which this liberation occurs remains fixed in its positions, the woman liberated by Don Juan is free only in the sense in which Marx speaks of the nakedness of the "free" proletarian. She finds herself with no recourse. Through her encounter with Don Juan she ceases to be a social slave, but she acquires no personal identity.[3] Women will have to struggle until the twentieth century before they will see the dawn of a freedom other than the negative freedom of earlier times, before they will be able to escape from the indeterminacy in which the seducer leaves them.

Thus Don Juan presents himself as a vehicle of liberation, since he himself is much more than a libertine. He is an agent of liberation, not a freedom fighter. He provokes or accompanies vast social upheavals without furnishing a collective model. And, just as he goes only part of the way with Elvire, he does the same with society. He does not battle to impose his way of life but just keeps on affirming his sole desire. Here we have a double bind: condemning Don Juan amounts to blaming the process by which man sets out on the path of freedom, but absolving him means giving up any hope of forming a free society, one that respects the other.

---

3. Montherlant's Anna de Ulloa is quite clear on this: "It is you who made me a woman. That is much more than having given birth to me. It is you who gave birth to me. [You are] my father, in so doing, doing this for my mother and for him. You, you did this for me."

FIVE

DISENGAGEMENT

$\mathcal{A}$ man without a name, a man of masks, possessed but not possessing, is Don Juan also a bad debtor? Sganarelle's cry, "My wages! my wages! my wages!" that provides the pathetic and terrible closing note of Molière's "comedy" seems to validate this claim. But are we dealing here with the unpaid bills of a penniless gentleman or with an aristocrat thumbing his nose at laws he considers beneath him? In the first case, Don Juan would inspire contempt, since he disregards ordinary people. The second case invites us to wonder about the meaning of such a denial.

If Don Juan is refusing to fulfill his monetary obligations, he hardly deserves our consideration. Of what philosophical interest is a dishonest person? Perhaps this is why, in Lenau's (1841) play, he pays up everything he owes just before he dies. If he has debts, they must be of another order. Would centuries have spent so much time on a figure guided by stinginess? If, on the other hand, Don Juan's action enables us to get closer to the heart of our culture, he becomes crucial to the understanding of modernity.

When Shakespeare writes, "Base is the slave that pays" in *Henry V*, he is referring to the great lord who brushes away the need to pay up. But the focus remains on the monetary debt. The prince is the one who does not pay. He spends, and his creditor is lucky indeed if he does not wind up in jail or condemned to death by way of reimbursement. We know of the kings of France and England—Philip II, so-called Augustus, or Edward III, for example—and their Italian financiers who were obliged to thank his lordship for sparing their lives in exchange for the cancellation of debts. Though not a king, Don Juan behaves like one. Pay? Who could bother? Respect a due date? Why stoop so low? In fact, he never pays up. Debt is his usual state. He owes, and that is all there is to it.

Duty involves two large categories of meaning: one has to do precisely with the idea of indebtedness, while the other has to do with having an obligation (cf. Malamoud 1996). Although the connection is often subtle in most Indo-European and Semitic languages (Benveniste 1969), there is an established relation between fault and duty (in the sense of the need for action). Certain languages have preserved the traces of this relation; the German *Schuld*, combining the two meanings, is a striking example. We must also distinguish the "duty" that impels action in the form of discharging a debt from the "duty" that calls for repayment. "I owe you two hundred francs" and "I owe my life to you" have neither the same meaning nor the same import. Likewise, "I owe my life to you" and "I owe my

66

soul to God" do not refer to the same type of debt. In the first case, I have contracted an obligation toward you, and perhaps one day I will have the opportunity to repay it. You and I are linked in an asymmetric relation that can potentially be transformed into a relation of equality. I owe my life to you, I save yours: a life for a life, and we are even. In the second case, I didn't ask to be born, and you tell me that my soul belongs to God. Fine! But on what basis? What is it, exactly, that I owe? What obligation does this impose on me? What is the nature of the relation that is created in this way?

These various meanings are often confused with one another, or at least mixed up, in approaching the question of Don Juan's debt. But we have to distinguish two very different kinds of debt, to which this figure maintains different types of relation.

Taking things one day at a time, Don Juan agrees that he is a debtor because he is constantly making commitments. He is fully aware of owing. However, this "owing" has to do with a debt contracted with regard to someone. At a more fundamental level, the level of "having an obligation," he recognizes no duty other than desire and its gratification. As usual, opposites coexist in Don Juan. The analysis of their cohabitation, once again, will give us a better understanding of the relation of this figure to exchange.

To acknowledge a debt and refuse to pay it is the position of a Figaro, who replies to Bartholo, "Do you doubt my honesty, sir? Your hundred écus! I would prefer to owe them to you for my whole life than to deny them for a

single instant," and often that of Don Juan, who says to
M. Dimanche, one of his creditors, "This is something that
I am not hiding, and I say it to everybody." He admits it,
just as long as he does not have to discharge the debt. This
is the key point: acknowledge, but postpone, shift the payment. "Shift" can be understood in its two complementary
meanings here: move back in time and twist the meaning.

The displacement in time, the *différance*, to use Derrida's
term, is Don Juan's preferred strategy. As he proclaims in
Molière, it's a bad policy to hide from your creditors; it's
better to pay them something, and he has the secret of send-
ing them away happy without giving them a penny. Put
off the due date, pay with empty promises—in short, always give without ever giving. But popular wisdom rejects
such a practice. Doesn't it proclaim that "giving and taking back are not the same thing"? Paying in words when
money is what matters, but also when other engagements
are involved, is a betrayal. Every promise, and especially a
promise of marriage, involves the same policy. "You who
pretend this way and trick women, death will make you
pay," is the way Tirso de Molina's Catalinón lets fly at him.
Don Juan replies, "That bill of yours does not fall due for
a long time." This offhand manner is not a ploy. When
Tisbea warns him, "This love had better engage you, and
if not, may God punish you," he responds in exactly the
same way, and the formula comes to his lips eight times in
the course of the play. If the debt does not fall due for a
long time, it is nonetheless real. "For there is no delay that
does not arrive, no debt that is unpaid," sings the Chorus
with Don Gonzalo. Now, what is it that happens at the

due date? That is a big question, one that leads us to an issue raised earlier, namely debt in the sense of "being under an obligation."

Let us consider the tragedy of Don Juan as a whole. A man deceives women by swearing his love and promising to remain faithful. On this account, all the protagonists tell him that he will have to pay one day or another for his misdeeds, whatever their nature. He mocks these warnings and follows only the dictates of his desire. A woman's scent sweeps away everything else. He is not afraid of incurring the wrath of God or man, because, he thinks, the due date is far off. Outside of time at each moment of his life, and thus perhaps eternal, he does not succeed in imagining the future. Or, to be more exact, guided by his impulses— something he is well aware of and perfectly happy about— he lives in the moment. He knows no restraint. But this is not the way everyone else understands matters. The norm must be respected. And so there is an additional element: not only does the due date, however distant, remain inevitable, but the death of the villain must restore the balance upset by his dissolute life. In other words, an insistent principle of equivalence is tacitly operating: *Esta es justicia di Dios: quien tal hace, que tal pague* (This is God's justice: an eye for an eye, a tooth for a tooth) is often repeated by Tirso de Molina. It is as though Don Juan's debts mounted to the point of overflow. He must die, certainly, but in such a way that his transgressions are exactly made up for. How? Hell will find a way.

Thus a finely balanced structure is set up, in which any deviation must be canceled out and every debt paid, regardless of the due date. Tirso de Molina's play establishes an inexorable symmetry. The ordering of life and death obeys a law that would later be called the law of communicating vessels. If the level rises on the right side, it falls on the left, and vice versa. No depression can last permanently; God or men will restore order. The former imposes a "grand equilibrium" and the latter pursue "small" ones. The large-scale equilibrium calls for a global and supreme compensation, at the end of which all debts are paid. Death settles life's accounts. On the small scale, there is a series of balances that every man must respect in the course of his life, independent of the grand equilibrium. For every passive there is an active, and vice versa. Every act finds its opposite. Moreover, popular wisdom repeats this in all ways and in every era: the happiness of some means the unhappiness of others; the last shall be first; justice will be done; ill-gotten property will do no good; laugh today, cry tomorrow; take your pitcher to the water too often and it will break; and so forth. If the series of small balances is upset, the large-scale one will finally establish itself and rectify everything, however far in the future the bill falls due. This is the condition on which peace is assured.

And so finding peace comes down to discharging one's debt to existence. All the great religions have inquired into how man might achieve this. The root SLM of *Islam* in Arabic is also found in *salem*, "peace," "to pay," "to achieve." Sibony (1992) notes that this root also has the meaning "submissive": in submission to Islam, therefore, all accounts are settled; the issue of symbolic debt is resolved. Christianity poses the question of redemption through the person of Christ and his sacrifice. Islam and Christianity are alike in this emphasis on the need to pay, to settle the debt originally contracted by each man, whatever his condition. Freud, too, often surmised that men feel the weight of an indefinable burden, associated with divinity, that can give rise to a guilt complex (cf. 1912–1913, 1927, 1939).

Salem in Arabic and *shalom* in Hebrew (from the verb *leshalem,* "pay," "discharge a debt") mean "peace" and "pay." Thus to be at peace means to be submissive or to have paid. In this sense, Don Juan is the archetype of the unsubmissive man. He will die without having paid his debts, and for that very reason will be unable to find peace. Unabsolved of his faults, he will know eternal damnation, hell. Just as he does not acquit his debts, the tribunal of God will not acquit him. Faithless in all senses of the term, that is, unpurified, he categorically rejects this sort of debt. What exactly are you saying to me, Don Juan thinks, when you appeal to heaven? It's a nice word, but all I believe is that two and two make four, four and four make eight! He has no logical or religious reasons for rejecting the fundamental debt that man contracts at birth. He denies the very idea of having to pay. But this does not prevent those around him from seeing in his damnation a rightful restoration of matters. The brave Sganarelle says so straightforwardly: "Everyone is satisfied by his death: heaven that was offended, laws that were broken, girls that were seduced, families undone, husbands driven to extremes, everyone is happy." And the valet adds, "Only I am unhappy, since, after so many years of service, I have no reward beside seeing with my own eyes my master's impiety punished by the most horrible punishment in the world. My wages! my wages! my wages!"

The structure of equivalence thus exerts its power, except for one thing. A sort of compensation does indeed seem to prevail on all levels—religion, society, love, lineage—but one detail escapes it: a corpse does not repay the money it owes! To be sure, whoever dies pays his debt, as Shakespeare wrote, but the cancellation holds good for the one who disappears, not for the one who remains. The settlement is not the same on both sides. The famous double-entry bookkeeping does not operate here. A monetary gap appears at the very moment in which Don Juan leaves the scene; no one will ever reimburse poor Sganarelle. And yet the fact that the valet will not get his wages is his punishment. After all, shouldn't he have left such a master, both to undo this solidarity and to avoid becoming its victim? In a certain way, the structure of equivalence ends up stealthily reasserting its rights. Sganarelle is punished for not having had the courage to leave a villain, even if the villain was his master. He must pay for that, which means not being paid monetarily. Thus, at the same time that compensation plays a role on the individual level for the valet, it also operates on the societal level, since, with the tragic death of the criminal, society can consider itself globally indemnified for the offenses it underwent. Sganarelle remains unpaid; society receives payment. The circle is closed because it does not close.

Has Don Juan ever felt the need to settle his commitments? On the contrary, he acts as though he could not care less. For Montherlant (1972), he says so quite unambiguously. The Commandant, like Tirso de Molina's Don Gonzalo, points out the rule, generally accepted and socially proven, that there is justice in heaven and on earth; every act must be paid for. Don Juan vigorously replies that there is no such payment. What does he have to pay for? The pleasure he had or the wrong he supposedly did? Paying for pleasure is fine with him; the pleasure women gave him was the highest pleasure anyone can give. But what wrongdoing was there? He made women happy. In the case of married women, why didn't their husbands satisfy them? As for virgins, he continues, the case was like that of soldiers who pillage the homes of their countrymen: if they didn't do it, the enemy would. With widows, he took care of the orphan; with nuns, he donated to their convent. To spinsters, he offered illusions. He taught the young to mature, as the sun does with fruits.

A fine plea in favor of asymmetry! Don Juan simply brushes away the socially required symmetry between his acts and their consequences. In his eyes, pleasure justifies any action. This freedom extends very far: if God is the ultimate creditor, Don Juan does not consider himself indebted, any more than with anyone else. He goes as far as to deny any obligation even to his own father. His is a supreme claim to freedom: I am no one's son, and God your father is not mine. I am what I am. Similar in this regard to the God of Moses, he could simply call himself "I am." Thus, in Molière, Don Luis shows his resentment in a long tirade in which he bitterly regrets having gotten from heaven such an unworthy son. Don Juan offhandedly suggests that he sit down. This is what is meant by not *paying attention*. Don Luis then goes along the same lines as Don Juan when he makes the terrible admission that the two of them do not get along well at all and are equally tired of one another. Don Juan's ancestors disavow him as their flesh and blood, Don Luis adds later on. He thereby puts him in the position of someone who founds a line. But, since he has no children (except in Montherlant, to be his manservant), Don Juan has neither ancestors nor descendants. The eighteenth century thus propelled this figure into a space of utmost freedom, making him the embodiment of the man in charge of himself. Orphaned and without issue, he reaches the height of isolation and pure individuality. He becomes free in the sense of a free particle.

This absolute freedom explains the relation between Don Juan and the notion of debt. Yes, he accepts his debts, because he constantly acknowledges them. But acknowledging a debt is not the same as paying it. He confirms, ratifies, endorses, but does not pay. At least, acknowledgment is his initial tendency, backed up by his words. At the same time, all his actions go in the direction of refusal. When it comes to a global indebtedness, in which the supreme creditor is God, Don Juan exempts himself. Duty? But what duty, and to whom?

Although he believes that recognition of a debt is equivalent to payment when it comes to men, when it comes to God he will not even say that a debt has been contracted. Though he admits that heaven can be *the* creditor, if that pleases the common run of mortals and society as a whole, he persists in the idea that this debt will remain forever unpaid. Thus he not only claims the right to behave as he wishes, he amply justifies himself. He argues on the grounds of an economy of sensuality that holds good for everyone. Every woman and every man, he maintains, can go beyond social rules and conventions, taking pleasure as a guide. He does not claim that this goes against marriage and human institutions in general, and, if he changes his mind, he does so only by way of a transient hypocrisy, especially in Molière. He undoubtedly prefers bargaining, exchange based on interest, to deceit. He knows that pride plays a greater role in the world than interest, and he also knows that this makes life complex. If men were guided by interest alone, Don Juan's would be an interesting scenario. But—along with pride—vanity, jealousy, and pretense dominate in human motivation. By this measure, Don Juan denotes, troubles, and ruptures codes. To live peacefully with his subversion, he talks, promises, plans, engages, but never stays firm. Is he a man of his word or just a man of words?

SIX

DISENCHANTMENT

Don Juan professes to believe only in arithmetic. Since two and two make four, and four and four make eight, the grand bookkeeping introduced by Pauline thought should be seductive to him. In the final analysis, even with a far-off due date, a balance ought to be evident. But arithmetic does not mean balance. As we have seen, Don Juan maintains two different attitudes, one with regard to monetary debts and another to the idea of the fundamental debt of life. Though ventures of the first kind may remain unpaid, the obligation toward the supreme creditor is of no concern to him. Where men are concerned, Don Juan does not so much refuse to pay his debts as knowingly confuse acknowledgment and payment. Where God is concerned, his religious blindness quite simply prevents him from seeing where the problem lies. Through these two complementary attitudes, he rejects any balanced transaction, any exchange of equivalents, any compensation whether immediate or indefinitely postponed.

Taken to its conclusion, the logic of equivalence postulates an iron law: whoever does not pay immediately, or quickly, will definitely have to pay up one day. As Tirso de Molina puts it in the *Trickster*, "*Esta es justicia de Dios: quien tal hace, que tal pague*" (This is God's justice: an eye for an eye, a tooth for a tooth). Thus, while in the human order a debt may potentially be left in abeyance, there can be no economic depression with God. This is Molina's final didactic message, defending and illustrating Christian truth. The play set out to make this a weapon against the possible weakening of Christianity; it undoubtedly achieved the opposite aim.

Does Don Juan measure himself against God? Certainly not. If he did so, this would mean that he accepts the idea of God's existence. Does atheism define him? Here again, no. First, he never professes any belief whatsoever, and atheism is a belief in that whoever does not believe in God inscribes his belief in the domain that he contests. Somewhat like the idea of critique in Kant, which is primarily defined in terms of limit, the circumscription of a field instead of any sort of negation of it, the atheist is situated within one of the possibilities that the believer makes available to him. Thus Don Juan never rejects the idea of God, an idea that is not in the least incompatible with the rules of arithmetic. If we follow Descartes, the mind of man and the laws of nature are organized according to the same norms, which makes their mutual comprehension possible without having to eliminate God. Each time that the words "God" or "heaven" are used against him, Don Juan accepts them without a moment's argument. And why, indeed, should transcendence bother him? It's other people's business, not his.

In Indian thought, Malamoud (1996) observes, the idea of an originary debt accounts for certain large duties to which man is obliged. This debt does not correspond to anything, any fall, sign, or contract, but from the outset it places man in the position of debtor. The sole fact of being born gives rise to a debit for a man, though he has not sought anything. This immediately suggests the analogy, mentioned above, between fundamental debt and original sin. But Malamoud draws attention to a crucial difference between the two themes. Original sin presupposes a contract: man sinned and must redeem his error. Debt here is clearly marked. In the other case, the debt called *rna* in Sanskrit refers to an immediate given of human life. And the absence of an etymology for *rna* argues for an absolute anteriority.

There is certainly a difference, then, but the concepts are nonetheless close on the level of daily human life. Whether it is the result of a contract or a state, there are three paths to freedom from this fundamental debt. The first is to settle up with the creditor all at once. When it is a question of life, one destroys oneself, and the repayment takes the form of a suicidal offering. The second way is to make payment in installments throughout one's lifetime; one has to "live with it," as the popular expression has it with regard to an illness one suffers. The last way involves placing oneself beyond the reach of the creditor, evading his grasp. In this case, the debtor denies any obligation and frees himself of his burden by taking flight. This flight enables him to escape the cycles of deaths and rebirths.

Although Don Juan's behavior does not reflect this last logic precisely, it is close to it. From the outset, he accepts the necessity of death without balancing it against life. Let us dare to conjecture that Don Juan wills his death. Not only does he know that he will have to die, which is a common-place, but he wishes this. His categorical refusal to repent (except in Tirso de Molina, where he expects to do so for a moment before changing his mind and dying without abso-lution) argues in favor of this conjecture. His philosophy leads him not just to flee death but also to desire it, not out of some morbid inclination or attraction to suicide, but with a clear and conscious will. Don Juan walks calmly toward the encounter with his death. He does not wish to die, but, since he knows the fate of man, his death wish makes it possible for him not to lapse into sadness or melancholy. What is most extraordinary about him, and perhaps closest to true heroism, is not that he accepts dying so easily but that he seems in no way to be touched by the idea of no longer living. Scorning death amounts to mocking what comes after it. Accepting that life will end involves organizing one's exis-tence in such a way that it will not arouse the least regret at any time. The fatality of death is received in contrary ways by men, and if some wish to approach it with open eyes, many flee its anticipatory signs. Agreeing with good grace not to live any longer entails true courage. In this small difference, which makes all the difference, lies the greatness of Don Juan.

Having peopled his sky with no divinity, he can neither converse with it, nor submit to it, nor seek protection, nor rebel. No supreme being inhabits the lands in which Don Juan makes his way. He is alone and will remain so. Can we even imagine him saddled with an *and*? Don Juan and Elvira, or Don Juan and Anna? That wouldn't seem right.

Faust has Gretchen, Orpheus Eurydice, Tristan Isolde, Romeo Juliet, Majnûn Laylâ, Pelleas Melisande. Don Juan is alone. Alone, but happy, we must never forget. He breathes optimism. When he gets up in the morning, he is sure that he will find new women and new pleasures. In the evening, he is confident about the next day and the unknown things and unknown women it will bring. At night, he perhaps dreams of women. He is, in fact, a great solitary who hates solitude. He starts the day by thinking how he can slake his thirst, and if he doesn't succeed right away, he doesn't imagine a permanent failure. The prospect of pleasure makes his pleasure endure. Don Juan is joyful before making love, and during, and after. Postcoital sadness is not for him. As he sees it, making love means not taking but giving. Here, as always, he expends. Taking can occasionally bring happiness, but one never gives sadly.

To know and not to hope presupposes a knowledge of causes and effects, but it also implies an absence of self-deception. We find no evidence in Don Juan of ignorance of reality or of lying when it comes to himself. He may lie to others, but he never tells himself falsehoods about himself. He knows quite well that death is waiting at the end of the road, or on the way, but this does not prevent him from living his life. He abandons himself to every excess, which is a sign of madness, but at the same time he assesses the consequences of his acts, which is a sign of wisdom. He acts like a happy man, ignorant of all the passion of an Augustine or a Tristan, passion that primarily means loving, not one's object, but love in oneself. Lacking a subject, this feeling is fatally oriented toward sorrow and suffering. The opposite is true of Don Juan. Society warns him that death will punish his disrespect of his commitments. Fine! In his view, the pleasure of the flesh has nothing to do with love but is an affirmation of freedom. Not in humiliation of the other, as Sade will propose, nor in self-abasement, as courtly love advocated, nor in the heightened suffering elevated by Sacher-Masoch to the level of a sexual pleasure in itself. For Don Juan, the absence of pleasure is tantamount to death. He thus stays clear of passion, which is close to death, so as to win the freedom of the flesh. Is it as a contemporary of Spinoza that he loudly affirms the right of his body and the need for joy? The sorrowful passions listed by the philosopher form a frightening sequence: "sadness, hate, aversion, fear, despair, remorse, pity, indignation, envy, humility, repentance, abjection, shame, regret, anger, vengeance, cruelty: Spinoza's analysis goes so far that, even in hope, in safety, he finds that grain of sadness that makes these into the sentiments of the slave" (Deleuze 1981, p. 39). And, in fact, none of these attributes pertains to Don Juan. We might even get a sense of this figure by ascribing their antonyms to him.

Is it, then, in anticipation of the doctrine of the rights of man that he claims the primacy of the body and its right to pleasure?[1] One does not *have* a body, he states; one *is* a

---

1. In a UNESCO publication, the biologist Henri Atlan (1998) devotes a brief and remarkable article to the human body considered as the subject of the rights of man. He develops the idea that the form of the human body is the distinctive sign of the humanity of a subject. This "small" observation has many consequences, often decisive ones.

body. The first freedom comes through the affirmation of and respect for this body. Negative reasoning proves it: every obstacle to individual liberty begins with the constraint of the body. Rape, torture, the punishment of masturbation, the death penalty, murder, imprisonment, and slavery bear witness to this claim. The twentieth century adds to this list the ban on abortion and the traffic in organs removed from children, not to mention the gulag, death camps, or "ethnic cleansing." The body is central to freedom, and this is what Don Juan keeps on crying out across the centuries in claiming his pleasure.

We may add that he never experiences a moment of guilty conscience. In the second essay of *On the Genealogy of Morals*, Nietzsche (1886) presents an analysis that is perhaps based more on intuition than on a careful and systematic examination of the history of moral and religious thought. Yet he is vigorous in presenting the idea that the restriction of innate freedom leads to a guilty conscience, the worst impediment in that it is not externalized but internalized. To go against freedom, anyone who deviates socially must be punished. The harshness of the punishment, Nietzsche notes in passing, is in direct proportion to the weakness of the community. A strong society even manages to protect the criminal from the vengeance of the masses. But man has gradually turned against himself inclinations formerly directed toward others. In this way he has developed an illness of the self, for a guilty conscience is truly an illness. Men imagine themselves indebted to their ancestral founders. The duty to discharge this debt through human sacrifice (Abraham's refusal symbolizes the condemnation of this practice) has perpetuated the idea of an obligation reinforced by a sense of duty toward the divine. This thesis sets forth the need for a liberation of conscience in order to attain freedom. Freud will add to it by showing that the process calls for a more profound individual effort along with an understanding of the collective ancestral practices that give rise to myths.

From Spinoza to Nietzsche and Freud, does Don Juan express the decline of this guilty conscience? Does he enable freedom to begin playing a role on the decisive level of daily life? Beyond good and evil, in those realms where the two philosophers assure us that our true life opens out, is Don Juan like an explorer discovering what is good and what is bad?

In contrast to good and bad, good and evil have to do with transcendence. Transcendence takes root in the ignorance of causality and thus imposes itself on men all the more easily. God willed it! May God's will be done! The Lord giveth, and the Lord taketh away! The invocation of the sacred, the inaccessible, the mysterious entails submission to the inexpressible and the divine. Tyranny, Spinoza says, persuades men that their salvation lies in loving their servitude, a notion dear to La Boétie and developed by him under a related aspect in his *Discourse on Voluntary Servitude* (1545). If men became aware of causes, they would refuse to submit and would seek what was best for them, not what was defined as good by an external, and hence tyrannical, power, whether political or religious. Understanding that the plague comes from a virus and not from divine wrath, for example, leads to a radical change in preventive measures. Since men's lives largely depend on their belief systems, these call for close examination. Now, in the Appendix to Book III of the *Ethics*, Spinoza (1677) explains how good and evil, these transcendent and for that reason alienating notions, poison men's lives. Sin and the accompanying need for redemption, but also fault, merit, and everything that might turn back against man, are condemned by Spinoza in the name of life.

Don Juan recognizes neither sin nor fault, neither good nor evil, in an absolute sense. For him, nothing exists on this side of life, and nothing beyond it. There is no remote or enchanted place underlying existence. Life on earth belongs to life on earth, and that is all. Nothing offsets anything. He is thus quite simply a stranger to the grand principle of symmetrical reciprocity anchored in Western thought. And the more he believes that two and two make four and four and four make eight, the less it matters that he denies the existence of God. In the current phrase, he no longer believes in transcendence and wants to hear only about immanence. This intellectual attitude may shock the advocates of transcendence, but he doesn't care about that. Is this offhandedness? Perhaps, but it can also be called courage.

Spinoza's defense of the existence and uniqueness of God does not prevent Don Juan, a stranger as he is to the divine, from adhering unwittingly to that philosopher's conclusions. For him, God remains a hypothesis necessary for some, useless as far as he is concerned but a kind of rumor without importance and in any case of no interest. This hypothesis does not lead him to take sides. Animated by no project, not seeking to reform society or any individual, he accepts it, as he does his debts, but in no way does he intend to conform to its social implications. Thus, when the Commandant holds out his hand during the feast at the end, he gives his own without hesitation. No fear is apparent on his face or in his thoughts, in contrast to all those who form his entourage and, already, his funeral cortege. It is as though Don Juan has been used to death for a long time, as though death entered him at the same time as life. The scene of the funeral masque envisioned by Montherlant illustrates this idea. Present from the beginning in the heart of the living man, death keeps growing within him. One day it takes form, becomes embodied: apart from the living man, it appears life-size, visible, free of its initial context. A separation occurs, and it can finally appear in broad daylight. Inhabited by his death, Don Juan is vaguely aware of this presence within him. He knows in some confused way that it will nonetheless have no effect on his attitude toward the world and toward God.

In taking the hand held out by the Commandant, is he accepting the restoration of the disturbed balance? Not in the least. The law of symmetrical exchange would require a compensation. And Don Juan refuses to settle accounts. He does not discharge his debt toward the Creator and maintains that he owes him nothing. What is demanded of him—here, his life—he does not pay but gives, relinquishes. He dispossesses himself of it, as he dispossessed himself of property and women. Hence the impression of suicide that we sometimes have when someone is little concerned to save himself. And, in any case, the debts remain unpaid. Even in dying, Don Juan has not acquitted his debts.

When Tirso de Molina embroidered a figure intended to reveal the greatness of God and the predominance of Christianity, history turned against the author. Don Juan has always played against type! Doesn't Molina, subverted by his creation, anticipate the theme of Frankenstein that was to preoccupy the West? Instead of confirming divine law and the imperative of divinity itself, Don Juan as an idea first acts on a subterranean level and then works his way up into the light to sap the foundations of this doctrine. Molina was prepared to utilize the resources of the supernatural in order to stress the need to submit to the power of God. Threats of divine wrath weigh heavily right from the beginning of the play, and they are actualized at its end. God is found at the beginning and the end of any action. But instead of this, the following centuries place onstage a figure who defies heaven, which cannot bend him to its will. The Don Juan of the seventeenth century represents unbelief punished, while from the eighteenth onward he affirms the decline of religion and the rise of the free individual. His refusal to repent sanctions the failure of God and, moreover, of hell: Would hell have had to be invented if God's omnipotence prevailed and converted men at every moment? Doesn't the very invention of that counterpart, the devil, reveal the stubborn concern to create a balance, a compensation, even in hell? Isn't killing a man because one hasn't gotten him to repent the act of a God who is pathetically at a loss for what else to do, already perhaps under the control of the devil, who is apparently his opposite but is in fact his twin or his clone? It may be objected that the damnation of Don Juan is clear evidence of divine punishment. Perhaps! But who has firsthand proof of this?

As for Faust, he expresses what Don Juan rejects. Goethe's (1787–1831) drama unfolds between heaven, where everything begins, and hell, where it ends. In the intervening period, the life of the hero is just an episode. He hopes to regain the sovereign good, the lost paradise, his youth, and in so doing he becomes involved with evil. Hence man's ceaseless dialogue with the devil and with God. Now, to accept that life is not a mere interlude between heaven and paradise or hell but a sufficiency unto itself, calls for great inner strength, a huge amount of character. A stranger to the logic of Faust, Don Juan experiences what Heidegger calls *Geworfenheit*, humanity thrown upon itself. While Goethe's hero wants to domesticate the devil and makes a wager with him that he imagines he can win, Don Juan draws up no agreement, signs no convention. He subscribes to the demands of his own life. He adapts himself to the world as best he can, with a smile on his lips and joy in his heart, without fear of damnation. And whereas other men, his contemporaries or not, are determined to refind a lost paradise, he feels no sense of loss. He seeks no tranquillity in "the peace of the Lord," since the world in which he lives is not an intermediate stage between two Edens. For him, to live is to experience pleasure. That is his "character," in the English sense so often emphasized by Orson Welles with his fable of the frog and the scorpion: not only the way one is made, but also the way one decides to be. His wager, which is no longer one, consists in preferring a bird in the hand to two in the bush.

In the famous passage from the *Pensées* devoted to the wager, Pascal (1662) assures us that the mathematical gain is infinite and the loss minimal. For this reason, he maintains, to bet on the existence of God is mathematically the best possible strategy. No doubt, but if the wager must lead to renunciation, contrition, and withdrawal from life, the loss is certain and the gain quite unpredictable. In addition, to wager in the sense recommended by Pascal presupposes certainty when it comes to God's expectations. To get to eternal life, we would have to be sure of what pleases him in order not to lose his favor. Now, haven't the variety of religious practices and the wars of faith across the centuries shown that God, if he exists, never manages to impose a law that is valid for everyone? No, Don Juan is definitely not going to amuse himself with this kind of wager. Or, more precisely, he has bet on the immediate certainty, pleasure. He establishes no correspondence between an expectation and a strategy. His actions know no aim but pleasure. The idea of profit and that of probability associated with the result are equally alien to him. He is already ahead just by playing the game. Don Juan does not bet rationally; his only concern in playing is the game itself. He is a true gambler.

PART III

OVERTURES/OPENINGS

SEVEN

A DEATH

If Don Juan had been wealthy, he would have lost everything by dying: body and property, that is to say, women and wealth. But he dies as a free man, in the sense that he is stripped of everything. He can thus face death without any caution whatsoever. Grasped by the hand of the Commandant, he knows that he is going to leave the earthly world, the society of the living. He gives himself up willingly to Hades, the god of the nether world. His descent to hell takes place with clarity of mind. The Commandant having honored his invitation, Don Juan in turn invites him to have dinner soon. Always in motion, always in a hurry, intolerant of slowness, he impatiently cries out to the statue, which defies him. Leporello tries a diversion: "Excuse him; he hasn't got time." Don Juan brushes away such a poor objection. Not only will he take time, but he will prove his courage. The statue insists: "Make up your mind," as though Don Juan were hesitating. But, on the contrary, his will does not waver for a moment. Everything is clear to him:

"I have already decided." In this a priori decision lies the suspicion of suicide mentioned above; this means that he has assessed the consequences of his acts. "Are you coming?" the statue continues gravely. After a final attempt by Leporello, who begs his master to refuse, Don Juan, self-assured, calmly agrees to go.

How to face death calmly if anxiety is clutching you, emotion flooding you, remorse gnawing at you? How to let go if the claws of life are gripping you? Since life is feeling and death absence of feeling, Don Juan is not concerned with death. In this, he is strictly Epicurean.[1] For him, death is not the price to be paid for life. It offsets nothing. What matters is not living for death but living for life and then dying. No symmetry is established. The concept of redemption, dear to Christianity, is not accepted here. Whoever grasps the hand of the Commandant as a sign of alliance with death in no way cancels out his life. The two worlds remain separate. With a calm heart and a mind at peace, Don Juan gives up life and nothing else.

Thus, when the Commandant orders him to repent, he can definitively refuse. In Da Ponte/ Mozart, this refusal is repeated six times. It is thus with full awareness that Don Juan rejects the Commandant's order, which amounts to an ultimatum. "No, no, it will not be said, whatever may happen, that I am capable of repenting," Molière's Don

---

1. In the letter to Menoeceus, Epicurus says that whoever fears death is a fool, not because he will suffer in the afterlife, but because he suffers needlessly at the thought of death's arrival. Death means nothing to us, since when we are alive, death is not there, and when death is there, we are no longer alive.

Juan declares to Sganarelle, without even a request on this point from the statue. In the *Trickster*, Don Juan almost gives in: "Let me call someone to receive my confession and absolve me," he begs, but he is told that his repentance comes too late. The priest Tirso de Molina apparently wanted to show the cost of not believing in divine wrath. The God of mercy is also a God of vengeance, absolution and revenge being the two symmetrical terms of a correspondence. Why, otherwise, would the idea of the last judgment have been invented? Don't heaven and hell form the two opposite poles of a huge equilibrium?

Don Juan does not repent in the end. Whatever the circumstances of his death, whatever the last words he utters, he departs from life and will discover the hell that the living promised him in their threats. What will he find, then? Damnation, the abomination of eternal suffering, the abyss of degeneration and despair? Will he have to endure the torment of a punishment meted out according to his wrongdoing? Will death be the reverse of life? If that were the case, wouldn't he have totally lost?

During his life, Don Juan does not tolerate symmetry. He opposes it not by believing in asymmetry but simply by behaving spontaneously. As we have seen, this general tendency is found in his relations with women, with property, and with God. It is also expressed toward death. The issue here is subtler, since death is perceived as the great cancellation, the meter reset to zero. Among the beliefs of the West there is the idea that death and life correspond to one another. We die as we lived, according to folk wisdom. The good go to heaven, and the bad will not escape hell. Measure for measure. This too is something for which Don Juan has no respect. It is thus very useful to see what happens right after his death, at the moment when, it would seem, the gates of hell open before him.

The fifteenth poem of the *Flowers of Evil* (Baudelaire 1857) can serve as a guide in these dark regions, since Baudelaire is the only author to have focused on Don Juan post mortem. His vision sustains the thesis of a figure who upsets all balance and symmetry.

When Don Juan descended to the wave beneath the ground,
And when he had surrendered his obolus to Charon,
A somber beggar, proud-eyed like Antisthenes,
With vengeful and strong arm he took hold of each oar.

Showing their pendulous breasts and their open robes,
Women writhed beneath the dusky firmament,
And, like a great flock of victims to be slaughtered,
They trailed on behind him with a lengthy wailing.

A laughing Sganarelle reclaimed his salary,
And meanwhile Don Luis, with a trembling finger,
Showed to all the dead wandering on the banks
His audacious son who laughed at his white brow.

Shivering in her shroud, the chaste and thin Elvire,
Next to her faithless spouse who was also her lover,
Seemed to appeal to him for a final smile
In which would shine the sweetness of his early vow.

Upright in his armor a massive man of stone,
Stood at the boat's helm and cut through the black wave,
But the tranquil hero, bent over his sword,
Watched the wake and did not deign to see all this.

[trans. S. F.]

The border has been crossed. Don Juan has just paid his toll to Charon. He finds himself in the company of an oarsman who inevitably recalls the beggar who is mocked in Molière's play. And what does he encounter in this sinister realm? Women, first of all, many of them, immodest, conquered even before having succumbed, but also all the people who helplessly stood by during his exploits on earth. Sganarelle, like Figaro, is quick to laugh at everything out of fear of having to weep at everything. Don Luis, the father grieving at his son's debauchery, can only display his impotence. As for Elvire, amorous nostalgia overcomes and paralyzes her. In the middle of this landscape in black and white, in which only laughter is heard, forced laughter no doubt, from Sganarelle, the statue of the Commandant pilots the terrible crew. At its edge, Don Juan. What is he doing? He fixes his gaze on the wake, which he sees as little as he sees the universe around him.

It is strange that the "tranquil hero," at the moment when he departs from life, immediately finds all the protagonists of his existence. What are his feminine conquests, Sganarelle, his father, and Elvire doing here? Why does he find them right after having been swallowed up in the night of the Commandant? A frightening apparition, this retinue he is trying to avoid. And yet, Don Juan does not change one iota and confirms his choice: he sees nothing, Baudelaire tells us. To new reproaches, he would reply with one more "no." Beneath his absent eyes, the wake forms a kind of thread linking the world of the dead to that of the living, but it closes over as quickly as it was formed.

The entire poem is situated in a liminal space. As in his lifetime, Don Juan is still in transit. The boundary between the world and the underworld has become invisible. Baudelaire calls him a tranquil hero. Why "hero"? Is he a hero in the Homeric sense, a warrior who speaks fine words and accomplishes noble feats? Obviously not. Is he a solitary man struggling against everyone else in the name of a higher moral truth? Again, no. Perhaps Don Juan's heroism stems from his fearless acceptance of death. He dies in a straight line, without shame, without remorse, without repentance. This self-confidence gives him a calmness that reveals his inner and outer involvement. He entertains no hope and goes forth without regrets into the infinity of hell. He pays no attention to Elvire, to the alluring women, to his father, to Sganarelle (who in any case would not believe it), or to the statue of the Commandant who got on board with him. Posted at the stern of the boat, with a faraway gaze: What he is dreaming of? Could it be that he is thinking of nothing? This would mean that he has been defeated by events, that he is being led along with no control over what he is experiencing. But this is not in character for him. Is he recalling his past life? Nostalgia is out of place in this figure. Is he withdrawing into himself in order finally to confront the absence of God? He agreed to die, but he did not give over his soul to anyone, quite simply because he does not believe in the soul. Beyond death a struggle continues. For to see nothing, to look at the wake at that moment, is to take a position. Don Juan remains mute, but he is the opposite of a blind man. It is not that he sees nothing; he *deigns* to see nothing. He could see, if he wished to, but then he would be taking a first step toward the repentance he had pushed away. Does he develop a guilty conscience about the humiliation and despair of his father? About Elvire's expectation? His debts to Sganarelle? That would be to return to his past and meditate on his errors: not the sort of thing he does.

Baudelaire's poem thus poses a strange question: Why does hell seem identical in all points to the world above? The dead "wandering on the banks" and the statue of the Commandant are side by side with the living figures of Sganarelle, Elvire, and Don Luis. Is Don Juan himself really dead? Are all these protagonists elements of a dream? Is this mixture coming from the unconscious? But if this is a dream vision, Don Juan will awaken. As in Mañara's story, has he merely dreamed his voyage to hell?

Another solution is to maintain that Don Juan, condemned to hell, must eternally relive his life without being able to change anything. He suddenly finds himself enclosed in a bubble that symbolizes an eternal present. We see this bubble from the outside, as it were, since we know about the damnation. But Don Juan cannot leave the bubble so as to view it in its totality. Having enjoyed life like no one else, he suddenly considers hell to be not its reverse but a kind of prolongation. An absurd but optimistic version of this infernal descent would be to think that Don Juan knows all this, that he accepts and maintains his positions on life, God, and death. A less optimistic version would be to say that he can't go against the fate that has befallen him and is resigned to it. He brings his memories with him, but he can change nothing. The boat's wake will distance him more and more from his life experience, without ever allowing him to forget it. His unhappiness will lie in his inability to alter anything.

In Baudelaire's depiction of Don Juan's new surroundings, we see a world over which the "hero" no longer has any control. Condemned to repeat each of his acts throughout eternity, he will come to know the rupture of time. This man who sought change in order to reach permanence is now confronted with the worst of constancies. From now on, instead of living in successive beginnings that are in no way to be confused with his dread of repetition, he is in danger of living only in eternally new beginnings. He discovers the other side of eternity. This perhaps explains his gaze fixed on the wake. Once again, death does not balance life but extends it in the same direction. Symmetry is indeed the sworn enemy of Don Juan.

This is surely why Baudelaire's imagination tells us that life, death, and hell are milestones on a continuous line, and hell is not the opposite of paradise. Believing in the symmetry of this man-made equation is not for Don Juan. A life cannot be paid for. Women have nothing to do with heaven, since only the renewal of seduction is heavenly. To win the favors of a new woman, each time, is delicious. To make love twice with the same one is depressing. To possess is to lose oneself. Don Juan cannot enjoy the same object twice in a row. Heaven is diversity. Hell is . . . whatever. But forever.

A *POESIS*

The theme of equivalence has slipped into this book. Whether it is a matter of God, death, women, property, or money, Don Juan always turns out to be off balance. Each time the law of symmetrical reciprocity tries to impose itself, he evades it. He himself, as we have seen, represents an asymmetry. Where the world demands balance and compensation, immediate or ultimate, he breaks the law. Once again, and through the negative, this behavior sheds light on the structure that Don Juan infringes upon. What is it?

Its most obvious expression is found in a human and social science that has continued to grow within Western thought, namely political economics. For at least two centuries, political economics has been promoting an invisible architecture of knowledge that it has, as it were, transformed into scientific truth. At the heart of this structure the principle of equivalence reigns supreme. It decrees that no commodity produced by men for the purpose of sale can be exchanged in society for a commodity of a different value. More precisely, this principle rests on the idea of a strict identity between the poles of any transaction. The great classical economists, chief among whom are Adam Smith, David Ricardo, and Karl Marx, consider labor to be the basis of value and the duration of labor its measurable content. Products, then, are nothing but crystallized labor. Beyond their different literary expressions and the variable order of their arguments, these economists founded a science of exchange entirely shaped by the principle of equivalence. In a transaction, they state, it is not goods that change hands but an equal labor that circulates. Apart from this sacrosanct rule there is no scientific salvation. Equivalence is not just the pedestal on which a thought is erected; it is formally the very principle of intelligibility. Marx is its prophet, explaining in his masterwork, *Capital* (1867), that no theft can occur in exchange, beginning with the theft of the proletarian by the capitalist. What the former sells on the market of use is not his labor but his capacity to work. As for the capitalist, he buys not labor but the power of labor. This is a decisive difference for Marx, since it enables us to understand how the exploitation of one man by another comes about. As with all commodities, it is possible to determine the "exchange value" of the power of labor, which depends on a certain work time crystallized in products necessary for the maintenance of this power and for its reproduction.

Thus the capitalist pays for labor power at its value, but spends beyond what would be strictly necessary for its reproduction. The difference creates a profit. This reasoning applies not only to the proletarian considered as a commodity but to all commodities. It underlines the extent to which the law of equivalence operates, but in the shadows, as if hidden behind appearances. Marx tracks it down in its furthest corners. In his correspondence with his friend Engels, he explains that the introduction of the difference between labor and labor power was decisive for him, since it enabled him to find in the heart of capitalism a mechanism operative in slave and feudal societies.

Thus, by dint of logic, a kind of historical invariant is confirmed: consider two objects, or any elements of a transaction, and you will not find any common point other than this powerful fiction, this idea, of value, itself a function of work time. In political economics, the two poles of exchange are always identical and interchangeable, or, to put it another way, equivalence naturally implies symmetrical reciprocity. It makes no difference whether we read a mathematical equation from right to left or left to right: the formula A equals B is strictly equivalent to B equals A. A perfect circular relation. Complete neutrality of a relation without bumps or hitches. You can take A for B or B for A, and no one will see a difference. Goods exchanged may differ in their physical appearance, but in terms of value nothing distinguishes them. In fact, they express the same value beneath a variety of phenomenal forms.

It took centuries to establish this reading of the social relation as ultimately based on exchange. Although it is possible to claim that the notion of balance was already present in the domain of physics, cosmogony, or medicine, even that it came from the Greek concept of *isonomia* as opposed to *monarchia* (cf. Vernant 1962), this was the first time that the thesis was so strongly asserted in a social analysis.

Is this enough to make political economics a more or less legitimate descendant of the divine rule of "an eye for an eye, a tooth for a tooth," or must we invert the proposition and consider that the history of social thought can be reread through the lens of political economics? Must we accept a latent correspondence between Paul of Tarsus and Marx? In any case, it is easy to find in each of them—that is, in thought in general and in economic thought in particular—the belief in an exact compensation between opposite terms. However far off the due date, eye for eye and tooth for tooth will be the law in life as in economic exchange.[1] A law that holds good at each moment and as a generalization.

This law conquered minds, in economics and elsewhere. The West is in thrall to it to the point where any deviation seems heretical to us and needs to be abolished, automatically if possible or, failing that, by an effort of will. If nature abhors a vacuum, society detests imbalance! Social man endowed with perfect reason flees any extreme. And so he becomes furious when he sees someone contravening the supreme law. And how much greater is his rage if, in addition, the person prides himself on unrestrained enjoyment of this wicked pleasure! Can we blame Don Juan for his

---

1. One might also add: nothing is lost, nothing is created, everything is transformed, according to the formula of Lavoisier, nearly contemporary with the great classical idea and participating in the same logic.

rebellion, then? Clearly, that is not where the issue lies. In his disobedience, he engraves all the more deeply the tradition he is trying to abolish. In opposing dogma, he highlights it. Like a stranger to his own culture, he accentuates its most salient features. At the same time, he prefigures the general attitude of the man of today.

Must we, then, look differently at this negative of balance that is Don Juan, look not with "modern" eyes but with those of a "primitive"? By this measure, wouldn't we be like him? If each of his daily acts violates reciprocal symmetry, our highest law, don't we have to seek another logic to reconcile Don Juan and society? Through the economy of the gift and return gift, for example?

For Michel Serres (1976), Sganarelle's introductory eulogy of tobacco in Molière's play declares balance to be the ideal: "From the outset, the law that will dominate the comedy, the law scorned at every turn of the plot, is prescribed on a small-scale model. How to become virtuous and a man of honor? By offering a gift before the request is made, by accepting and receiving" (p. 234). Giving and receiving is the fundamental law set forth in the play.[2] For Serres, the logic of the gift and the return gift explains *Don Juan* entirely. But we must be clear about what is involved here.

Don Juan never returns anything. He does not pay back. In the face of invective and threats, he takes flight before-

---

2. Beaumarchais' (1775) Figaro notes that the secret rule for being a courtier can be summed up in three words: receive, take, request.

hand. When creditors demand their due, advances or wages, he replies with words or with his absence. Through his own displacements, he keeps on shifting the terms of a possible exchange, precisely rejecting the logic of the gift and return gift. In one case, the scene with the pauper in Molière, he briefly requires compensation: I will gladly give you alms, but you have to take an oath! This is a typical contradiction, since charity is defined as being outside the realm of compensation; it is a gift pure and simple. But charity operates on two levels: it enables the giver to derive personal gratification (whether narcissistic, altruistic, or egoistic makes no difference), while the receiver gets a little money to live on. It is therefore not in the category of a gift, in the sense Derrida (1991) has in mind when he writes that, as soon as the other accepts, as soon as he takes, there is no more gift. The interest of the dialogue between Don Juan and the pauper is that, for the first and only time, someone doesn't succumb to the seducer's charm or his reasoning. That Don Juan finally gives the coin "for the love of humanity" is a sufficient sign that he could not care less about compensation or reciprocity. The only time, then, that he agrees to play the balance game, he has fun with it. This is additional proof of his heresy. He gave for nothing. And this is what he always does, giving and receiving like everyone else, to be sure, but for nothing. His mental space is defined by gratuitousness. He keeps on playing this one game of his, ignoring the emphasis placed on exchange by economics and accountancy. Everything he does is gratuitous. In the way he moves, he buys only one-way tickets and haughtily ignores the return trips. Does this inscribe his acts in an economy of the gift, as Serres believes? Again, we must not view the gift through the distorting lens of equivalence.

Ever since Mauss and his famous *Essay on the Gift* (1925), ethnologists, historians, philosophers, sociologists, and economists have wondered about the manifestations of an exchange in which the symbolic and/or imaginary aspects take priority over any other aim.[3] Unfortunately, the idea of a return gift that balances the gift usually indicates a retroactive projection of the thinking of political economics where it would be more sensible to get free of it and, especially, more useful to forget it. Despite the uniqueness of the *potlatch*—that gift in which the spirit of the thing given is never reduced to the material offering—current thinking has been too quick to compare "primitive" exchange with a certain type of calculated economic exchange. In a manner of speaking, equivalence has promoted to the rank of certainty a mental straitjacket that tends to find symmetrical reciprocity in every transaction. Of course, many ethnological studies of primitives and of peoples closer to us show the circulation of goods or of "necessary generosities" (as Duby [1973] says in regard to the Middle Ages), but this does not prove that such flows come about under the influence of calculation. To be sure, the return gift corresponds to the gift as the basis of social relations and their capacity for reproduction, but why insist at all costs that the second gift is the counterpart of the first?

---

3. Beside Serres and Derrida, one could cite Lévi-Strauss (1949), of course, but also Baudrillard (1976) or Godelier (1996).

Why introduce the idea of a *return* gift where *another* gift simply confirms the prior one? Why tack on symmetry where its absence would bother no one? I give to you, you give to me, I receive, I give again, you give again: there is a circulation, but your actions will never compensate for mine.

There can be no doubt that reciprocity is a human invariant. The *potlatch* studied by Mauss makes sense only if one gives back more, that is, if the two gifts remain unequal. Here again, this is true as long as we recall that inequality is not based on a calculus or an economic measurement but corresponds to a nonmathematical estimation of the importance and the spirit of the thing given. Gifts are mutually consecrated but never cancel each other out, whether they are taken one by one or viewed as a whole over time (see Rachline 1991). The idea of an offering giving rise to its counterpart is quite simply foreign to this system. To grasp how this asymmetry works, imagine a present that a gift in return would "balance." How could we say that the "sum" of two opposite acts of generosity ends up as zero? Who would maintain such a foolish notion? If I must offer in turn, as a sign of acknowledgment, I will do so as best I can, but how can I say that this second gesture annuls the first one, of which I am the recipient?

There may certainly be reciprocity in all this, but not symmetry. Instead of equivalence, there are depressions, discrepancies, gaps, openings. The *moka* and *potlatch* identified by ethnologists participate in this logic, a logic that, in *The Accursed Share*, Georges Bataille (1949) justly sees as important, though with little effect. He determines that in Aztec society, for example, bloody sacrifices are evidence of what he calls "consumption," that is, expenditure to no purpose. This example is surely not characteristic of all human societies, and it is even possible, as Godelier (1996) notes, that this is an exception, a product of a social mechanism that has gone mad.[4] But exception and madness are appropriate to Don Juan, since it is in the framework of an economy of pure expenditure that he is inscribed. God, women, money, time, and death are occasions for him to tear away the veil of symmetry. He lives solely in such openings. While the whole world demands equivalence in the manner of political economics, or compensation in the manner of the economy of the gift, he takes pleasure in the discrepancy.

Doing without expectation of return belongs to a logic radically different from that of self-interested action. While the latter presupposes a calculation—I do this so that you will do that—the former is gratuitous in nature. Don Juan does everything graciously, in all the senses of the term. He does not take; he gives. He does not exchange; he proceeds in one direction. And besides, what could anyone give him that would appease his appetites? He is fully himself only in action. If he speaks, if he promises, he does so first and foremost in order to be free to pursue the chase. His words are diversions. Not for him a wait-and-see approach: if he has to wait, it is only to heighten sensuality. In the game

---

4. Godelier is severely critical of Bataille's approach in generalizing these practices to humanity as a whole. He sees examples like the *potlatch* as less common than examples of gifts and reciprocal gifts that are offered to cement alliances, as opposed to extending the rivalry of individuals and groups.

he develops, he certainly hopes for reciprocity from the women he courts, but by definition it cannot be symmetrical. He generates a "maybe" but doesn't care about a counterpart, let alone an exact one. He has to keep moving. He *acts*. He does not love; he *makes* love. He does not think; he *does*. He does not pay; he *makes* debts. With women, everyone knows what he *does*.

It may be useful here to recall that the word *poetry* comes from the Greek *poiësis* (the Latin form is *poesis*), meaning "action of doing," pure creation, and thus, at the same time, loss. As Bataille (1949) observes, the term *poetry* is applied to ordinary states of loss, perhaps with the connotation of expenditure: it thus means creation by means of loss. In that sense, Don Juan's economy belongs to the world of poetry.

EIGHT

GIOVANNISM AND MODERNITY

*H*is scorn for all compromise when it comes to symmetrical reciprocity locates Don Juan in a rationality that has been repressed by the triumph of the concept of balance. Four centuries have not always paid tribute to his philosophy—on the contrary. Once again, we may note a peculiar similarity between this conceptual figure and an iconoclastic twentieth-century author, Georges Bataille, in which Don Juan is the ancestor of Bataille and goes beyond him. In approaching the notion of expenditure, Bataille (1949) tries to show that consumption always represents a moment in the cycle of production, while expenditure has to do primarily with loss. Loss interrupts a process as much as consumption renews it. It is a break, an action with no purpose but itself. In contrasting this "principle of loss" to the "principle of classical utility" that shines in the firmament of traditional economics, Bataille is stating the irreducibility of the one to the other. Let us go further. While the one has to do entirely with a strict accounting, in which each act finds compensation, the other defends the idea of inexhaustible differences. On one side equilibrium, on the other discrepancy. There balance, here its absence. Two diametrically opposite worlds. Two irreconcilable worlds. But two worlds that are nonetheless interrelated.

The former is unquestionably the dominant one, but Don Juan traces the uncertain contours of the latter. The lineaments of modern man can be discerned behind his general attitude. We see this in his relation to time and in his claim to freedom.

For Don Juan, time is a complex matter. Why is he restless? Is it for sheer distraction, a way not to think of his condition; or self-denial; or is it an acknowledgment of his nature and an affirmation of life? Is he seeking above all to escape boredom, as Baudelaire thought, or Montherlant, who has him say that he would rather die of beheading than of boredom?

The theme of inconstancy is familiar from the sixteenth century onward. It is one of the ingredients constituting the figure of Don Juan in the wake of poets like Marino.[1] In the view of Pascal (1662), man struggles to forget that he is man, and he is to be pitied less for his ontological inconstancy than for giving himself over to play and entertainment in order to distract himself. In contrast, Montaigne (1595) is not annoyed by inconstancy; he celebrates it. For, he says (Book III, Chapter 2), constancy is just a more sluggish

---

1. An Italian poet of the sixteenth century. His poem *Amor incostante* (*Fickle Love*) begins with the instructive lines, "Do you want to see / A new Proteus of Love / And a new Chameleon?"

oscillation. The notion of inconstancy has its roots in Heraclitus; beyond Montaigne it extends to Nietzsche and, more generally, to all philosophers of joy and the saving laugh. It advocates life and the enjoyment of our stay on earth, since we die only once and, as Molière says, for a very long time. Don Juan feels that imperative. He savors existence the moment it is offered to him. Taking advantage of every opportunity, he consumes life and burns the candle at both ends. It is as though he were saying, with Montaigne (Book III, Chapter 3) that to live from day to day, and for himself, is the sum total of his plans.

In his study of time, Georges Poulet (1952) questions this claim, since it is one thing to locate oneself in the present, another to stay there. The fear and hope inherent in ordinary people revive the past or project into the future, but they turn away from the present. Taking hold, capturing, is thus the only way to belong to oneself, to be one's own over time, while every moment evaporates and we are constantly overstepping the bounds of the present, inspired by a future that prevents us from enjoying immediacy. This capturing, then, is a matter not of possession but of making one's own. How totally Don Juan! Besides, there would be no use in seeking to possess, since time is continually escaping us. To make one's own is to dive into the present, as Epictetus recommended long ago, not in order to forget oneself but, on the contrary, to live fully in time. The capacity to delimit the present, as Hadot (1986) says with regard to Marcus Aurelius, consists precisely in removing everything that could get in the way of our taking hold of it as best we can.

For Don Juan, each woman is a present, in both senses of the term: gift and immediate pleasure. A succession of presents forms the substance of his life. And yet, hardly has he immersed himself in one when another is already on the horizon. He never manages to locate himself in any particular present and remains unable to dwell in any. For him, chasing a woman amounts to orienting each of his presents toward future presents. But this procession has no continuity. It is as though Don Juan did not exist in the interval between two presents. Or, more exactly, he exists only from the point of view of a present to come. His mental universe is on a slope. And so are his presents. He does not know that straight present that Horace wished for when he proclaimed his famous *carpe diem*. His motto could be: "He who does not seduce, passes on," since "pass" means both "to die" and "to fall into the past."

The pleasure of the senses—eating, drinking, smelling, smoking, hearing, looking, making love—does not slake the thirst of Don Juan's existence but gives him the opportunity to take hold. Like Montaigne, he aims to halt the swiftness of the passage of time by the swiftness of his capture. The only way he can savor the eternity of a second of orgasm is to begin over again as many times as the body will allow. Sexual pleasure thus results not from a successful chase but from a chase that is forever being renewed. When Montherlant's Don Juan exclaims that he is pursuing permanence in change, what he is expressing is not despair over inconstancy but delight in ceaselessly repeated beginnings. Can this quest come to an end? Can we imagine a permanent feast? Can sex itself offer such constancy? Montaigne (1595) writes:

When I imagine man besieged by desirable delights—let us put the case that all his members should be forever seized with a pleasure like that of generation at its most expressive point— I feel him sink under the weight of his delight, and I see him wholly incapable of supporting a pleasure so pure, so constant, and so universal. In truth, he flees it, when he is in it, and naturally hastens to escape it, as from a place where he cannot stand firm, where he is afraid of sinking. [p. 511]

In spite of this typically despairing observation of Montaigne's, Don Juan does not keep himself from enjoying sexual pleasure or from beginning the search for a new pleasure as soon as the present one is over. Above all else, he hates the whole *horror vacui* of which Nietzsche spoke. He therefore tries to dwell in time by getting rid of everything that could stand in the way of his doing so. He must not possess or become attached to anything—to objects, of course, or to women.

In this ceaseless quest for permanence, he differs from other men only in his courage, since he entertains no hope of success. Perhaps in this way he approaches heroism. His obstinacy makes him a brother to Sisyphus, though he is unlike him in one small, but essential, detail. The mythical hero behind his rock surely knows of the final failure, but this does not prevent him from beginning anew all over again. As Camus (1942) says, we must imagine him to be happy. But Don Juan does not repeat the same action indefinitely. Each time, he makes love in general and in particular. In the first case, there is repetition of the act, in the second a systematic renewal. We do not envision Don Juan making love two times in a row with the same woman. But to make love with a different woman each time is to go beyond repetition, since no woman is ever like another. This is the nature of the connection between his inner time and social time. As René Char says in connection with poetry, Don Juan's life is a fulfilled desire that remains a desire. Once again, he personifies the impossible.

In laboring to outwit boredom, men arrive more quickly at the very limit they want to do away with. The religious man can find some comfort in the "return" to God, but what about the unbeliever or the agnostic? They must draw from within themselves the strength to live without hope in an afterlife. They walk along a narrow ridge bordered by the precipices of despair and renunciation.

As Mircea Eliade (1963, 1971) has explained, men in certain so-called primitive societies were able to rediscover the presumed immobility of the earliest times by devoting their lives to rituals. Terrified of history, they refused to ascribe an intrinsic value to it. Time had to be conjured away. Does Don Juan share this feeling, and is he seeking to annul the passage of time by multiplying his feminine conquests? Through what utterly profane means does he regain access to the sacred? Are the chase, the capture, and the abandonment all part of a ritual that provides him with the illusion of suspending the flow of time? This is unlikely, since Don Juan does not deceive himself. He believes in concrete time, does not think that suffering can be a divine punishment, loves the unknown and thus loves stories, and is under no illusions about either men or society. Fleeing repetition like the plague, he does not for one minute believe in the myth of the eternal recurrence. He combines in one person the vision of Montaigne, for whom pleasure constitutes the final goal, and the vision of Camus, for whom the absurd is the spiritual substance of existence. In this way Don Juan rejects the closure associated with balance. He is, truly, unbalanced.

We have to take this last term in a broad sense. Don Juan's attitude is that of a man leaning forward. Not only does he never stay in one place, but any fixed present becomes unbearable for him. He keeps on pursuing that one sublime little moment that comes about through the ecstasy of love but evaporates even as it surges forth. That delicious instant that is offered by the body and that cancels out the body at the very time it is offered is what Don Juan relentlessly hunts. Thus his relation to pleasure is exhausting. Epicurus says of death that it is not when we are and is when we are not. Similarly, pleasure appears only when we abandon ourselves. Don Juan knows this. The rest is tactic or strategy directed toward this point.

Time for Don Juan, therefore, is an inextricable mixture of movements and instants. If he runs roughshod over the present in a kind of false *carpe diem*, he does so in order to jump immediately over to another present, destined to undergo the same fate. He thus brings forth a cascade of presents, each following closely on the last. In their midst, potential futures spurt up in fountains. A woman, a perspective, a pleasure. Another woman. . . .

Like Don Juan, the man of today traverses the present as though it were a stage toward an awaiting future that he has to reach for. His present is oriented, under tension. Everything must hang together in accordance with an inexorable law, the law of leaning toward the future. This is also a general inclination that nothing and no one escapes, which makes modern man a *giovannist*[2] and Don Juan his precursor. Both are sucked into that black hole of the future always to come, that inaccessible vanishing point toward which days and nights pour forth, and both succumb without really knowing how or why. The unknown attracts modern man the way every unknown woman fascinates Don Juan. Adventure, discovery, movement, anticipation, conquest: these form the intellectual atmosphere of modernity. Giovannism has become our horizon.

Society condemns this figure and at the same time preserves him in splendid isolation: If his ruptures and openings were granted citizenship, wouldn't the state sink into anarchy? And, in fact, his transgressive behavior opens up breaches that have social consequences. The most significant of these concerns the individual. Don Juan has removed the individual from the surrounding dross. The woman is transformed into a person free of her body; the man becomes his own master alongside a God who is, to be sure, still possible but no longer necessary. Both emerge from their chrysalis. Is the modern individual therefore a natural child of Don Juan? Probably, to the extent that this figure's libertarian claim paves the way for the era of the individual and, later, the growing affirmation of the sub-

---

2. The term *donjuanism* has too strong a connotation of seduction. The neologism is better suited to my conceptual aim.

ject, from Montaigne to Freud. Like a free particle bombarding an atomic nucleus, Don Juan has unleashed a formidable energy.

The presence of giovannism in the contemporary world, however, gives official recognition not to a triumphant theory but to the propagation of practices. Desiring, obtaining, savoring, discarding, beginning again: Doesn't our relation to material objects today recall the pursuit and the propensities of Don Juan? Isn't it like the seducer's constant wandering? The person who throws himself into an endeavor of any kind—economic, artistic, political, or any other—assesses his pleasure primarily on the basis of the movement that animates him, not on the outcome of his work. Someone once asked Gandhi whether the end justified the means. The Mahatma replied, "The end is *in* the means." So it is with giovannism, which expresses the mixture of ends and means.

A surfer, modern man experiences this confusion. A nomad, he constantly jumps from one image to another. As in electronic games, he knows several lives, intertwined or successive, exclusive or complementary. Staying in one place terrifies him. Speed fascinates him. He does not resist the attraction of novelty. If the channel surfer lives on flash and gets high on dazzle and suddenness, the web surfer navigates the internet and embarks each time for an unknown destination. Both pursue. Both refuse to grasp. They resolutely opt for transient captures. The channel surfer slides from sensations to impressions. Reality blinks before his eyes. The web surfer wanders about. A mosaic of worlds forms his universe. Meshing, branching, linking, alliance, interconnection: practices in which the plunge into the network aims not for possession but for movement. Whoever tries to possess will be sidelined. The images are found but not kept. Both the channel surfer and the web surfer are more or less groping their way along. In truth, they are poaching. They vaguely know what they want, but they don't know what lies ahead. On the lookout for novelty, they anticipate an unusual new capture each time. That is the hallmark of their giovannism. Explore, lie in wait, trap, exploit, slip away: how similar to Don Juan!

But we must be clear on certain points. Don Juan's greed, insatiable by definition, is a sign not of ignorance of reality but, on the contrary, of his acute awareness. The true giovannist is not deceived by a society in which the worst horrors and the noblest aspirations lie side by side every day. He knows the despair of misery and the distress of poverty, but this does not prevent him from seeing the emptiness of consumption thirsting for itself. He sees the world as it is. Though he transforms existence into a perpetual banquet, he has no illusions and hopes for nothing. He feasts and transfigures life. His feast is one of engagement, not conclusion. He needs exaggeration, perhaps in order to stifle the despair inside him. His present must be a celebration. It is a choice. He thus accepts the wager of his ancestor and clone, Don Juan himself. If a giovannist can assert himself today, then, it is through these tendencies, in which he acknowledges the disorderliness of the contemporary world and, at the same time, its inexhaustible potential.

CODA

There is no defense of a thesis in the behavior of a giovannist, just a vital affirmation. Don Juan promotes loss and gratuitousness. Equivalence is alien to him. Though he attaches importance to reciprocity, he scorns symmetry. Does he symbolize an aberration of reason or the beginnings of a subversive mode of thought? Does he embody social progress or the impossibility of any collective venture based on individual demands alone?

Don Juan cannot ally himself with anyone. His encounters never result in connections. He nips in the bud any potential relationship. The negation of permanence that produces his temporal continuum allows him no social recognition. At the same time, he succeeds in prefiguring some of the behaviors characteristic of the man of today. What frightened his contemporaries seems acceptable to his epigones. Those who consider Don Juan dead or outdated do not perceive his subtle topicality. Perhaps they confuse disappearance and invisible presence.

But who would seriously dare to claim that Don Juan represents a model for us? His wager has no stake. He plays for the sake of playing. He plays by himself, with others, with society. In so doing he makes a game of everything. He is a dubious precursor and an inimitable prototype, the one competing with the other. While the former partly announces the future, the latter is firmly pushed back to the margins of modernity. The spiritual destiny of this figure corresponds to his profound nature, in which attraction and repulsion are mingled without nuance. In telling us what we are not, he calmly continues to tell us who we are.

POSTSCRIPT TO THE
AMERICAN EDITION: DON JUAN
AND ECONOMIC CIVILIZATION

&ver since his birth, Don Juan has traced the outlines—vague outlines, to be sure—of a subversive economy. The shadow of this figure continues to infiltrate into the very heart of our mental and material universe, sometimes discreetly, sometimes without inhibition. The imaginary has permeated reality.

This book is an attempt to detect in the contemporary West the signs of a subtle presence and perhaps of a significant, if unsuspected, influence. It ventures into regions that have been insufficiently explored, regions in which there resound the echoes of a diffuse *giovannism*. Three of Don Juan's main features will be our guidelines: the concern to dispossess, the horror of identical repetition, and the major importance of the promise.

The economic civilization in which we live is based on the accumulation and retention of goods. If you lack possessions, you are worthless. The underprivileged aspire to

the status of consumers, despite the great and vague distance that separates them from the Promised Land. Having is quite naturally confused with being: whoever has, is;
whoever does not have is nothing; and whoever is nothing
does not exist. Nowadays, Diogenes would undoubtedly die
amid general indifference at the bottom of an old rotten
barrel.

This model, which arose in the great period of the In-
dustrial Revolution and was expanded along with a rampant capitalism, continues to govern our world and our
minds. And yet, at the same time in which the life span of
a cycle of consumption is getting shorter and shorter, the
more the production of things increases and the less time
they last. From the paper tissue to the plastic water bottle,
from the syringe to the tablecloth, from the beer can to
underwear, from cotton to the razor, the throwaway is
honored. Get it, enjoy it, get rid of it: these are the three
master verbs from now on. The unbridled pursuit of material
gratification never lets up and reaches all strata of society.
The growing popularity of renting, which is gradually re-
placing ownership and its expenses, highlights this phe-
nomenon. The most relevant country here, the United
States, is first of all a "renting country," not a "buying country." Thus the consumer craze is magnified, since renting
allows for the enjoyment of the goods of this world as though
one were staying briefly at a hotel—and all the better if the
lodging is a palace! The consumer society induces each of
us to jump from one object to another without even real-
izing what we are doing. Desire, obtain, savor, discard,
begin all over again: Doesn't the current relationship to

things remind us of the direction in which Don Juan is heading? Isn't it like the seducer's compulsive roving? It is this irrepressible inclination that I have suggested we call *giovannism*.[1]

What holds true for the result of the activity—the goods put at our disposal—is also the case for the initial undertaking of a project. In all the grand adventures of capitalism, the patrimonial endpoint has not mattered so much as the game, the will to power, or the wish to leave one's imprint. Profit has only a limited appeal for the true builders of empire, the military conquerors, the political visionaries, or the captains of industry. If action were motivated merely by the assessment of its quantitative result, few major projects would see the light of day, as was once pointed out by the great British economist John Maynard Keynes. The entrepreneur is like the gambler who speculates, even when the scant hope of profit should logically hold him back. (There is no question here of the administrator, who is so ignorant of the meaning of creativity.) In his quest, the entrepreneur is never a miser or a collector; he pursues the satisfaction of his desires and seeks pleasure the way the seducer does. But whereas the erotism at work in the case of Don Juan passes through sex without being reduced to it, the erotism of the entrepreneur takes another path, without being confined to it. For isn't the entrepreneur "enterprising," as we say of the seducer? Among the legendary capitalists, from the Buonvisi to the Fuggers,

---

1. *Giovannism* applies to men and women alike. I do not restrict it to one or the other sex.

the Rothschilds to the Pereires, the Carnegies to the Rocke-
fellers, from a Rupert Murdoch to a Bill Gates, none can
be defined in terms of the money and property amassed.
Their fortunes fascinated their contemporaries, who were
a bit too quick to confuse the visible result with the underlying motive, since the motive for the creation usually remained poorly understood. The creator plants trees; the
common person sees only the fruit.

This attitude is characteristic not only of the entrepreneur in the general sense but also, and increasingly, of
modern man, this *homo internetus* who is a web surfer and
a channel surfer at the same time. For both, the danger lies
in staying in one place. Things have to be kept in motion,
otherwise they're dead—and they're death. Every possession slows down the process, blocks it. What is important
is to get, not to keep. And in any case, the transaction has
more and more to do with a commodity of a particular sort,
information, which can hardly be conserved.

For all economic goods, with the precise exception of
this one, one person's gain is another's loss, and vice versa.
If I am cultivating a piece of land, or fashioning an object,
or intent on studying a file, I will not become simultaneously involved in another task. If I drink this glass of
water or eat this piece of bread, no one else will be able to
have it. At the moment when I am consulting this doctor
or attorney, neither of them will be available to anyone else.
When I receive this sum of money, it will not fall into someone else's pocket. In short, while labor, physical goods, services, and capital obey the same law, information disregards
it. The former, not the latter, are zero-sum games: one per-

son gets everything, the other nothing, or vice versa. Between these two extremes every possible combination is imaginable, but the sum of possessions will always remain the same. On the other hand, if I confide a secret to a friend, I do not forgo it; both of us are its guardians. Neither of us can lay claim to ownership.

Transactions involving information are thus positive-sum games. No exchange takes place on the basis of equivalence, since all those who take part end up winners. I give to you, you give to me: no balance is established, because as soon as you give to me, you set in motion a process that cannot find exact compensation. Reciprocity is at work, to be sure, as is always the case in social relations, but it is never symmetrical. Strangely enough, the predominant economic theory has not yet considered this issue seriously. Is it afraid for its life?

Information is really what channel surfers and web surfers are after, these two emblematic figures of the modern individual. Hungry for excitement, they are incorrigible *giovannists*. They both know what they want, but they don't know what awaits them. On the lookout for novelty, they hope to catch hold of something out of the ordinary each time. And this search casts doubt on whether acquisitiveness is really the prime motive for action. Does the person who navigates the web possess anything? He or she enters into contact, explores, and plays, but never amasses. Or, more exactly, his or her pleasure has nothing to do with accumulation. Attracting. Distracting. Developing strategies to capture the flow. Producing, possessing, and hoarding hold little interest. Tracking down the intensities is what counts.[2] Thus Don Juan is a starting point for the modern desire for enjoyment linked to exchange, to the unhoped-for, to the unknown, to discovery. But only on condition that the pleasure of the unexpected never be destroyed by identical repetition.

Reproduction, multiplication of the identical, is precisely the great ambition of societies that have profited from standardized capitalism. The first concern of the entrepreneurs of the nineteenth century was to ensure mass production. How could they eliminate breakdowns, get rid of interruptions in the processes of production, so as to feed an increasing and diversified demand? Taylorism responded to this challenge by reducing the possibilities of production and opening out onto the so-called consumer society. In the twentieth century, automation and robots have succeeded in taking control in this regard. They have even pushed logic to its extreme: in many cases man has become a hindrance to production. Less exact, less skillful, less reliable, less steady, less durable than the first robot on the scene, he gradually finds himself playing second fiddle. Without him, more and better production would be possible. For making an exact replica millions of times over, he is not the best solution by a long shot. Today's machines are able to fulfill all the conditions for perfect duplication;

---

2. In an earlier work (Rachline 1991), I developed the idea that an economy consists primarily of the capture of the signs of wealth and not in the connection between production and distribution.

man, on the other hand, makes mistakes, forgets, neglects procedures to a greater or lesser degree, and just goes on repeating his errors. Fortunately, his work is becoming increasingly dedicated to precisely what cannot be duplicated, what cannot be reduced to iterative procedures. Indeed, human intelligence seems to try hard to get rid of what is annoying, and nothing is worse than doing the same thing all the time. Laziness, the precious ally of intelligence, protects him from this. The history of human genius could be summed up as the will to get free of everything that repeats itself.[3]

Wind, animals, wood, water, coal, gasoline: this is how man gradually freed himself from obstacles to his horizon. Soon the mastery of solar energy will undoubtedly enable us to cross a new threshold. It will be yet another small step in clearing away repetitive tasks from man's doorway, so that he can get involved in other adventures of the mind. This is by far the most positive aspect of technical progress, which makes it possible for us to imagine man released from any hindrance to his creative genius. To each according to his ability: to machines mass production, to man the art of the singular. In the wake of this division of labor there may

---

3. One example among a thousand is little Humphrey Potter, one of the many children employed to inject cold water periodically into the tank containing steam, so as to ensure condensation in the first steam engines of the eighteenth century. It occurred to this young boy to use a pendulum to connect the faucet regulating the inlet of steam to the one regulating the output of cold water. This crucial advance allowed James Watt to perfect his engine, and, more important, the lad was able to play marbles instead of standing in one position for hours on end.

perhaps arise an economy based on man, alongside the one that is concerned with the production and distribution of goods. In the future, humankind may well be able to subjugate the economy instead of being subordinate to it.

Don Juan rejected possession and repetition in all their forms. At the end of the twentieth century, as we have seen, the dominant social practices echo this tendency. The priority accorded the promise adds a third element to the *giovannism* that has become so popular. This behavior, too, preoccupies the contemporary world. Two major domains in which the notion of the promise has taken over reality prove this out: money and the very nature of economic activity.

Elsewhere (Rachline 1993) I have described the eventful history of relations between money and capitalism. It turns out to have taken several centuries of fiscal evolution for the societies of the West to set up institutions capable of regulating the desired volume of currency. Breaking with millennia of enforced submission to nature, capitalism invented pure money, dematerialized, detached from any metal. In the course of history, however, the metal that worthy people placed on deposit with money changers and bankers always guaranteed the pieces of paper given in return. The banknote first bore the signature of its owner and then became payable to the bearer. Paying meant changing the banknote into its metallic equivalent, the rate generally being set by the lord. With the appearance of central banks, that is, monetary and financial institutions usually owned by the rulers (whether monarchs or representatives of the people), the conversion of banknotes to metal gradually became impossible. Between the very end of the eighteenth century and the second third of the twentieth, inconvertibility of funds became the norm all over the globe and under all forms of government. Nowadays a banknote is always inscribed on the debit side of the central bank, since it is payable by the issuing bank to the bearer. We have here a logical oddity: the banknote that I am holding in my hand is merely a promise on the part of the bank that issued it, but this promise is in itself a means of payment. In other words, it is a debt of the bank with regard to the economy and, at the same time, a claim of the bearer on that institution. When we settle our exchanges with banknotes, we pay one another with debts to us on the part of the central bank. But these pledges will never be honored, since they are backed up by nothing but themselves. All a central bank has to do is place in circulation debts to itself, and this promise without hope of fulfillment is instantly changed into a means of payment. Only public authority benefits from this privilege, denied as it is to the ordinary mortal and severely punished by the law, as banknotes often remind us. Just like Don Juan, the central banks can proclaim that their debt "is something that they do not hide and that they announce to all the world," since the signature of one of these financial institutions at the bottom of a piece of paper is all that is necessary to transform this piece of paper into a means of payment. For a central bank, acknowledgment of debt amounts to money. Don Juan behaves in exactly the same way. For him, too, a promise takes the place of the thing promised. The institutionalization, in the twentieth century, of the creation of money ex nihilo thus bears an amazing resemblance to an individual practice imagined in the seventeenth: an odd presence of *giovannism* where it was least expected.

The promise that remains a promise thus acquired a fine title of nobility by gaining supreme fiscal power. And this is not all. Such a promise is found today at the very core of economic commodities, where it breaks up a traditional dyad.

To take in all of world economic history in a single bold glance, it could be said that two major types of commodities have long characterized human activity: physical objects and provision of services. Weapons, instruments of daily life, buildings, simple or sophisticated agricultural implements, machines, and in general all material goods comprise the first category, which is historically the larger and more ancient. Alongside it we find a set of activities grouped together by virtue of their immateriality: worship of deities, the spread of a body of knowledge, political functions, the guarantee of protection against an enemy, artistic creativity, medical consultation, advice, and in general everything that remains intangible although of some utility. If we were to mark on a straight line segments proportionate to the relative influence of these two categories of wealth, material goods have represented the larger segment for a long time. Yet from the most remote epochs of human history up to the present, the cursor has been constantly moving in favor of the provision of services. The twentieth century has seen the irresistible increase of this latter type of asset.

For thousands of years material elements constituted the major part of human productions, and for about two centuries the already rapid growth of immaterial elements has been accelerating. Today market activity is crossing over into an additional phase. A third category of economic goods is becoming more and more influential: aleatory promises. These are conditional pledges whose execution depends on circumstances. Insurance is the best known case. To secure himself against a risk, the insured arranges for a policy or a premium in advance, and, if the event occurs, the insurer bears the expenses arising from the accident. This type of reasoning then extends over many domains, from stock options received by an increasing number of wage earners to television networks' selling of an audience to advertisers. But the sudden emergence of this marketing technique is especially notable in the financial area. Ever since the early 1970s there has been a spread of so-called byproducts, direct objects of transactions.[4] Henceforth it is promises themselves that are exchanged, independently of their fulfillment. Say that I have obtained a call on the dollar that will allow me, come what may, to obtain the currency at the prearranged rate. I can transfer this aleatory promise at any time, well in advance of the due date of the contract. In this case, the transaction will involve the promise itself and not the hope it represents.

---

4. These are immaterial assets associated with products, supporting these products (which may also be immaterial, like interest rates or exchange rates, for example), and giving rise to transactions. Options and futures are the best known types; an option is a right, exercised or not, and a future is a firm commitment.

Thus economic operations take place without ever materializing. Intangible but quite real, they are not at all superfluous or artificial and perform incontestable services, especially protection against contingent risks or against exploitation of fluctuations in securities. They are a sign of the progressive shift of market activity in the direction of a particular form of the real, namely, the virtual. In piggybacking on itself, as it were, and forming the matter of exchange, the promise gives rise to an economy that Don Juan would surely not have disowned. Thus the miracle comes to pass in which action becomes concrete by sole virtue of its projection into the future. How can we not recognize here, as in turning away from possession and going beyond repetition, the presence of *giovannism*?

––––––––––––––––

The three main lines of thought developed in this postscript add to the idea that sex is in no way sufficient to describe Don Juan's behavior. If that were the case, libertinism would have summed up his journey, and he would no doubt have remained on the sidelines of history. The pursuit of bodily pleasure alone would not have been enough to transform him into a conceptual figure who might teach us something about the way our society has evolved. If he continues to be of interest to us, it is because his temperament is not limited to what we might call an erotics restricted to sex but opens out onto a general erotics of life. Thus in many respects he prefigures the relation that women and men of economic civilization have with reality.

A WORD ABOUT THE
BIBLIOGRAPHIES

———————

$\mathcal{N}$owadays, Don Juan is mainly known as the title character of an opera composed by Mozart in 1787 with a libretto
by Lorenzo Da Ponte. And yet he came into being in the
sixteenth century under the pen of the Spanish monk Tirso
de Molina, whose real name was Gabriel Tellez. This man
of the cloth wrote over one thousand plays, but it was his
Trickster of Seville, in which Don Juan appears, that won
him a lasting reputation.

Since that time, a number of authors have been taken
with this figure and have brought him back to life across
the centuries in literature and art. Don Juan has been the
subject of plays (one of the most famous of which is by the
French dramatist Molière), novels, poems, films, ballets,
sculptures, paintings, and philosophical essays, not to mention studies of the psychoanalytic sort.

And yet the theme of Don Juan seems at first to be in-
credibly banal. Crazy for women, all women, attracted by
the slightest glimpse of petticoat, he will do anything to
succeed. He seduces both noblewomen and peasants, tall
and short, beautiful and ugly, old and young. This is all he
thinks about. Then one day, while he is trying to achieve
his goal with a pretty noblewoman in a townhouse in Seville

(which he has entered secretly), the girl's father, a Commandant, intervenes. In the course of a duel, Don Juan kills him and flees. People are running after him and looking for him, but he could not care less: all he can think of is his next orgasm. His valet, like a faithful servant, shields him from a society that predicts a dire punishment for him. And indeed, soon thereafter Don Juan finds himself face to face with the statue of the Commandant. The ghost asks him to dinner, that is, he invites him to die in payment for his dissolute life. Don Juan accepts right away. The Commandant threatens him with Hell if he does not repent. Don Juan bravely refuses, and he disappears in the course of this sinister feast.

It is this plot, briefly summarized, that has given rise to an extensive output of works of all kinds in the past four centuries. The list of references below contains only a sample of these, one that I hope is the most representative.

REFERENCES

Atlan, H. (1998). Agir pour les droits de l'homme au XXIe siècle. Unpublished paper, ed. F. Mayor in collaboration with R.-P. Droit. UNESCO.

Bataille, G. (1949). *The Accursed Share: An Essay on General Economy*, trans. R. Hurley. New York: Zone, 1991.

Baudelaire, C. (1857). *The Flowers of Evil*, trans. J. McGowan. New York: Oxford University Press.

Baudrillard, J. (1976). *Symbolic Exchange and Death*, trans. I. H. Grant. London: Sage, 1993.

Beaumarchais, P. C. de (1775). *The Barber of Seville*, trans. B. Sahlins. Chicago: Ivan Dee, 1998.

Benveniste, E. (1969). *Indo-European Language and Society*, trans. E. Palmer. Coral Gables, FL: University of Miami Press, 1973.

Blanchot, M. (1969). *The Infinite Conversation*, trans. S. Hanson. Minneapolis, MN: University of Minnesota Press, 1993.

Borges, J. L. (1967). "From Someone to No One." In *A Personal Anthology*, trans. A. Kerrigan, pp. 118–121. New York: Grove.

Caillois, R. (1938). *Man and the Sacred*, trans. M. Barash. Westport, CT: Greenwood, 1980.

Camus, A. (1942). *The Myth of Sisyphus and Other Essays*, trans. J. O'Brien. New York: Vintage, 1991.

Casanova, G. (1788). *History of My Life*, trans. W. R. Trask. New York: Harcourt Brace & World, 1971.

Dacunha-Castelle, D. (1996). *Chemins de l'Aléatoire*. Paris: Flammarion.

Da Ponte, L. (1787). *Don Giovanni, Libretto in Two Acts*, trans. W. H. Auden and C. Kallman. New York: Schirmer, 1961.

Deleuze, G. (1981). *Spinoza: Practical Philosophy*, trans. R. Hurley. San Francisco: City Lights, 1988.

Deleuze, G., and Guattari, F. (1991). *What is Philosophy?*, trans. H. Tomlinson and G. Burchell. New York: Cambridge University Press, 1994.

Delteil, J. (1930). *Don Juan*. Paris: Bernard Grasset.

Derrida, J. (1991). *Given Time: I. Counterfeit Money*, trans. P. Kamuf. Chicago: University of Chicago Press, 1992.

Descartes, R. (1637). *Discourse on the Method of Properly Conducting One's Reason and of Seeking the Truth in the Sciences*, trans. F. E. Sutcliffe. Indianapolis: Hackett, 1998.

Duby, G. (1973). *The Early Growth of the European Economy*, trans. H. B. Clarke. Ithaca, NY: Cornell University Press, 1978.

Dumézil, G. (1977). *Les Dieux-Souverains des Indo-Européens*. Paris: Gallimard.

Eliade, M. (1963). *Aspectes du Mythe*. Paris: Gallimard.

——— (1971). *La Nostalgie des Origines*. Paris: Gallimard.

Epicurus. *Letter to Menoeceus*, trans. R. Waterfield. San Francisco: Chronicle, 1994.

Foucault, M. (1976). *The History of Sexuality, Vol. 1: An Introduction*, trans. R. Hurley. New York: Vintage, 1990.

Freud, S. (1912–1913). Totem and taboo. *Standard Edition* 13:1–161.

——— (1927). The future of an illusion. *Standard Edition* 21:1–56.

——— (1939). Moses and monotheism. *Standard Edition* 23:1–137.

Godelier, M. (1996). *The Enigma of the Gift*, trans. N. Scott. Chicago: University of Chicago Press, 1999.

Goethe, J. W. von (1787–1831). *Faust*, trans. W. Arndt. New York: Norton, 1976.

Hadot, P. (1986). "Le présent seul est notre bonheur": la valeur de l'instant présent chez Goethe et dans la philosophie antique. *Diogène*, January–March.

Homer. *The Odyssey of Homer*, trans. R. Lattimore. New York: Harper Perennial, 1967.

Jabès, E. (1991). *Désir d'un Commencement. Angoisse d'une Seule Fin*. Paris: Fata Morgana.

Kierkegaard, S. (1846). *Either/Or. Part I*, ed. and trans. H. V. Hong and E. H. Hong. Princeton, NJ: Princeton University Press, 1987.

Kofman, S., and Masson, J.-Y. (1991). *Don Juan ou le Refus de la Dette*. Paris: Galilée.

Kolitz, Z. (1995). *Yossel Rakover Speaks to God: Holocaust Challenges to Religious Faith*. Hoboken, NJ: KTAV.

La Boétie, E. de (1545). *The Politics of Obedience: The Discourse of Voluntary Servitude*, trans. H. Kurz. Montreal: Black Rose, 1977.

Lenau, N. (1841). *Don Juan. Ein Dramatisches Gedicht*. Leipzig, 1921.

Lévi-Strauss, C. (1949). *The Elementary Structures of Kinship*, trans. J. H. Bell. Boston: Beacon, 1969.

Malamoud, C. (1996). Article: "Dette." *Encyclopédia Universalis*.

Marañon, G. (1942). *Don Juan et le Donjuanisme*. Paris: Gallimard (Idées), 1967.

Marx, K. (1867). *Capital: A Critique of Political Policy*, trans. B. Fowkes. New York: Random House, 1981.

Mauss, M. (1925). *The Gift: The Form and Reason for Exchange in Archaic Societies*, trans. W. D. Hall. New York: Norton, 2000.

Mérimée, P. (1910). *Les Âmes du Purgatoire*. Paris: Gallimard (La Pléiade), 1951.

Molho, M. (1995.) *Mythologiques. Don Juan. La Vie est un Songe*. Paris: José Corti.

Molière, J.-B. P. (1665). *Dom Juan and Other Plays*, trans. G. Gravely and I. Maclean. New York: Oxford University Press, 1989.

Montaigne, M. de (1595). *The Complete Essays of Montaigne*, trans. D. Frame. Stanford, CA: Stanford University Press, 1957.

Montherlant, H. de. (1972). *La Mort Qui Fait le Trottoir (Don Juan)*. Paris: Folio.

Nietzsche, F. (1886). *On the Genealogy of Morals*, trans. D. Smith. New York: Oxford University Press, 1996.

Pascal, B. (1662). *Pensées: Notes on Religion and Other Subjects*, ed. L. Lafume, trans. J. Warrington. New York: Dutton, 1967.

Poulet, G. (1952). *Studies in Human Time*, trans. E. Coleman. Westport, CT: Greenwood, 1979.

Rabelais, F. (1534). *Gargantua and Pantagruel*, trans. P. A. Motteux. New York: Knopf, 1994.

Rachline, F. (1991). *De Zéro à Epsilon. Economie de la Capture*. Paris: Hachette.

———— (1993). *Que l'argent soit, capitalisme et alchimie de l'avenir*. Paris: Hachette/Pluriel, 1996.

Rougemont, D. de (1970). *Love in the Western World*, trans. M. Belgion. Princeton, NJ: Princeton University Press, 1983.

Rousset, J. (1990). *Le Mythe de Don Juan*. Paris: Armand Colin.

Serres, M. (1976). *Hermès I. La Communication*. Paris: Editions de Minuit.

Sibony, D. (1992). *Les Trois Monothéismes*. Paris: Seuil.

Spinoza, B. (1677). *Ethics*, ed. H. R. Parkinson, trans. A. Boyle. London: Dent, 1989.

Tallemant des Réaux, G. (1653). *Historiettes du Grand Siècle*. Paris: Amis de l'Histoire, 1969.

Tirso de Molina, G. (1625). *The Trickster of Seville and the Stone Guest*, trans. G. Edwards. Warminster, UK: Aris & Phillips, 1986.

Vaillant, E. (1959). *Monsieur Jean, Comédie en Trois Actes*. Paris: Gallimard.

Vernant, J.-P. (1962). *The Origins of Greek Thought*. Ithaca, NY: Cornell University Press, 1982.

Winter, J.-P. (1998). *Les Errants de la Chair. Etudes sur l'Hystérie Masculine*. Paris: Calman-Lévy.

OTHER WORKS CONSULTED

Apel, K.-O. (1994). *Ethique de la Discussion*. Paris: Cerf.

Augé, M. (1982). *Génie du Paganisme*. Paris: NRF-Gallimard.

Barrès, M. (1986). *Du Sang, de la Volupté, et de la Mort*. Paris: UGE, "10/18."

Bazin, A. (1985). *Orson Welles*. Paris: Ramsay.

Berveiller, M. (1961). *Eternel Don Juan*. Paris: Hachette.

Bloch, E. (1991). *Le Principe Espérance*. Paris: Gallimard.

Brecht, B. (1984). *Don Juan*. Paris: L'Arche.

Buber, M. (1986). *Judaïsme*. Paris: Gallimard "Tel."

———— (1995). *Le Chemin de l'Homme*. Paris: Editions du Rocher.

Byron, G. G. (1994). *Don Juan*. Paris: Florent Massot.

Cervantes, M. de (1998). *Don Quichotte*. Paris: Diane de Selliers.

Cioran, C. (1990). *La Chute dans le Temps*. Paris: Gallimard "Essais."

Da Ponte, L. (1991). *Don Giovanni*, trans. V. Bianchini. Paris: Costallat.

Dautremont, C. (1981). *Grand Hôtel des Valises*. Paris: Galilée.

Droit, R.-P. (1998). *La Compagnie des Philosophes*. Paris: Odile Jacob.

Frisch, M. (1980). *Don Juan ou l'Amour de la Géométrie*. Paris: NRF-Gallimard.

Gaston Grangier, G. (1995). *Le Probable, le Possible, et le Virtuel*. Paris: Odile Jacob.

Gauchet, M. (1985). *Le Désenchantement du Monde*. Paris: Gallimard.

143

Gendarme de Bevotte, G. (1911). *La Légende de Don Juan*. Paris: Hachette.

Grant, M., and Hazel, J. (1973). *Gods and Mortals in Classical Mythology*. Springfield, MA: Merriam.

Hammel, J.-P. (1994). *L'Homme et les Mythes*. Paris: Hatier.

Hegel, G. F. W. (1992). *Principes de la Philosophie du Droit*. Paris: Gallimard.

Hocquard, J.-V. (1978). *Le Don Giovanni de Mozart*. Paris: Aubier.

Lévinas, E. (1984). *Difficile Liberté*. Paris: Le Livre de Poche, "Essais."

——— (1990). *Dieu, la Mort, et le Temps*. Paris: Le Livre de Poche, "Essais."

Lévy, S., and Lévi, O. (1993). *Genèse-Bereshit. Commentaires de Rachi*. Paris.

Macchia, G. (1990). *Vie, Aventures, et Mort de Don Juan*. Paris: Desjonquières.

Marceau, F. (1985). *Casanova ou l'anti-Don Juan*. Paris: Gallimard.

Massin, J. (1979). *Don Juan, Mythe Littéraire et Musical*. Paris: Stock.

Obliques, *Don Juan*, double issue 4 and 5. Paris: Borderie, 1978.

Pushkin, A. (1993). *Le Convive de Pierre*. Paris: Babel.

Rank, O. (1990). *Don Juan et le Double*. Paris: Payot.

Renaut, A. (1989). *L'Ère de l'Individu*. Paris: NRF-Gallimard.

Rosen, C. (1978). *Le Style Classique. Haydn, Mozart, Beethoven*. Paris: Gallimard.

Rousset, J. (1968). *L'Intérieur et l'Extérieur*. Paris: José Corti.

Schneider, M. (1994). *Don Juan ou le Procès de la Séduction*. Paris: Aubier.

Servier, J. (1991). *Histoire de l'Utopie*. Paris: Gallimard, "Folio-Essais."

Zeise, F. (1998). *Don Juan Tenorio*, trans. R. Daillie. Paris: UGE, "10/18."

INDEX